TED
AND THE
KENNEDY LEGEND

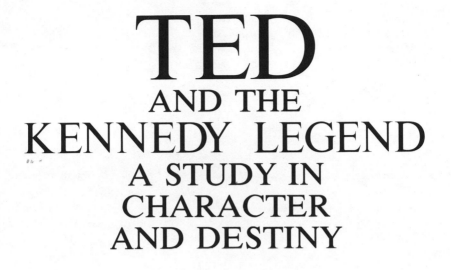

TED
AND THE
KENNEDY LEGEND
A STUDY IN
CHARACTER
AND DESTINY

by
MAX LERNER

St. Martin's Press New York / A Lawrence Field Book

Library of Congress Cataloging in Publication Data

Lerner, Max, 1902-
    Ted and the Kennedy legend.

    1. Kennedy, Edward Moore, 1932- 2. Kennedy family. 3.
Legislators—United States—Biography. 4. United States. Congress. Senate
—Biography.
I. Title.
E840.8.K35L47   973.92′C92′4 [B]   79–27300
ISBN 0–312–79043–0

For Jenny
and our sons
and the web of our years together

Also by Max Lerner

CONTENTS

FOREWORD

T HIS ISN'T a campaign biography, nor in the slightest degree
an official one. Neither is it one of those valuable detailed life
stories based on hundreds of interviews and sources. Those have
been done, and done well, and are available.

My purpose has been to do an analytical book, using the
material already there—almost too much—and suggesting a
frame within which this thrice-told tale may take on fresh meaning.

I have studied and known all three of the Kennedy brothers
in the way any historical observer does, distantly but with fascina-
tion. Over the years I have written more than enough about them.
Along with others I have been attracted and even haunted by
them.

But I am neither a Kennedy enemy nor a Kennedy groupie.
My concern is to see them in the large as one of the interesting
and important family clusters of political leaders in American
history, ranking with the Adams and Roosevelt clans. To take Ted
and his family *seriously,* as part of the enduring stuff of history,
is the final compliment a writer can pay his subject—with empa-
thy, perspective, detachment.

That perspective has been built into me by the mental habits
of decades. Thus, while I have sought out everything I can about
Ted and the Kennedys, I have also drawn on my own memories,
conversations, and writing over the past thirty and more years,
since John Kennedy first began to be known and "the family"

began to engage the public mind and psyche. I have tested old memories, reading, and assessments by more recent knowledge, and revised my judgments when later ones made more sense. At several points I have embodied brief passages from my commentaries written when the events took place.

Two decades ago, in 1960, John Kennedy—the first Kennedy to offer himself as candidate—was elected President, fulfilling the first phase of the Grand Design that his father, Joseph P. Kennedy, had initiated for his sons. After less than three years of his term he was assassinated.

Five years later an incumbent President, Lyndon Johnson, was challenged by the next brother, Robert. He too was assassinated before the end of the primaries campaign, and thus cheated of his chance to pick up the fallen standard of his brother.

After a little more than a decade another incumbent President, Jimmy Carter, was challenged for the Democratic nomination by the youngest and only surviving brother, Edward, bent on attaining the White House and living out the family destiny.

Thus the story of Ted Kennedy goes back through two earlier presidential campaigns and two deaths. "Very deep is the well of the past," wrote Thomas Mann. The Kennedy theme is a grand and classic one, quite unlike any other in American history—of ambition, striving, triumph, tragedy, destiny, myth, eternal recurrence, and their strange entanglement on the stage of American life.

The focus of this story is Ted Kennedy himself, the center of a web of relations and circumstances. I have tried faithfully to trace his life development. It is a hard field to traverse because it is filled with traps, land mines, bramble bushes and quagmires, and an overlay of fantasy and political theater. But there is another story also, since the Kennedy phenomenon is part of our time and place—the story of American power and how it is shaped by the media and the mythmaking process, and by the readiness of the American people to respond to the Kennedys out of a hunger for greatness.

There is no dearth of able books on the Kennedys—on the patriarch, on the President, on Robert, and several on Ted with considerable biographical detail. I add another because, like the mountain to be climbed, the challenge of the Kennedys is *there,* and Ted, as the surviving brother, is a good takeoff point. It is not a "life and times" in the sense of a formal full-bodied biography: I mean it to be more reflective and interpretive.

Yet it can't help dealing with Ted's turbulent life and its encasing era, his involvement with the triumphs and tragedies of the Kennedy family, his own pattern of intimacy relations on which there has been more gossip than serious writing, his inner world, the rise and decline of his political fortunes.

Whether Edward Kennedy ever attains the presidential goal or not, his story presents a venture in a number of areas. My own stress is on the role of family and elites in the American political structure, the relation of eros and power in the dialogue between leaders and people, how character is formed in the developing life history and how its strength or vulnerability is tested in crises, how political myths are fashioned, and the hold they exert on the people's minds and fantasies in a presidential system.

I write this *currente calamo* in the midst of the running stream, before the outcome of Ted Kennedy's 1980 presidential campaign is fully known. There are obvious dangers in doing so, but I have stayed clear of prediction and fortune-telling. There may even be some advantage in trying to catch the bird on the wing, to seize the nation in the act of sizing up a Kennedy again and deciding his political fate, while it copes with one of the most powerful political legends in its history.

There is a note of sadness here in the most recent phase of Ted's story, as there was a note of tragedy in some of the earlier phases. I have dealt with the affirmative elements—his creativeness as a Senator, his political courage, his capacity for survival, his resilience. Yet even for one who is not a Kennedy partisan it is painful to trace Ted's unclaimed presidential opportunities in the past, his effort finally to act out the family legend in a burst of resurgent energy, the frustrations he encountered, and the unraveling—at least for the present—of what was earlier a powerful mystique.

The reader will find that I have been severe with Ted, perhaps a bit unsparing, where he deserved it. But looking back at the story I think of Othello's cry, "O the pity of it, Iago, the pity of it."

Max Lerner
New York City
March 18, 1980

ACKNOWLEDGMENTS

I OWE MUCH to Rita Kupsick Katz, for research on the book and its photographs, and for her devoted skills and insights; to Evelyn Irsay, my executive assistant, for easing my path at every step as drafts became a book; to my seminar on the Presidency at the Graduate School of Human Behavior, U.S. International University, at San Diego, and especially to Dorothy Healey, for research help; to Hugh Hefner, for a decade and more of conversations about power and Eros, both of which are linked with the Kennedys; to Thomas McCormack, for being a good publisher; and most of all to my wife, Edna Albers Lerner, for an editorial scrutiny at once exacting and creative. As with every book I have written, I owe a debt to my continuing dialogue with her and with our sons, Michael, Stephen, and Adam Lerner.

CHAPTER I

PRIMAL FATHER AND BAND OF BROTHERS

1/The Family: Rooted and Invented

2/Joseph Kennedy's Grand Design

3/Patriarch, Great Mother, Band of Brothers

1

The Family: Rooted and Invented

— 1 —

A TV SET in a living room somewhere in America, in the spring of 1980. A family group gathered around it for the early evening news roundup. The network editor has put together his menu for the viewer—snippets of the day's events, lasting thirty seconds or a minute or two.

A man flashes on the screen, talking to an audience. He is big, husky, vigorous, with a ruddy face, a mop of curly hair, a broad jaw, a strong, sonorous voice, an arm stretched full length as his finger punctuates the mounting inflection of each sentence. He looks like a handsome Irish cop Harvarded up for the occasion, his frame bursting out of his well-groomed clothes. He is bigger than life, with an energy that makes everyone else seem pallid. Behind the easy charm he exerts there is a strong animal vitality.

He has a comedian's sense of timing, getting the laughs he wants. He is angry as he attacks the oil company profits or the draft registration, or as he describes the inaction of his target, the President, in the face of skyrocketing inflation. By long campaigning, he knows how to stir the crowd, even some who are indifferent or hostile.

Yet behind the outward air of confidence and humor there is the lurking sadness of defeat—the first major defeat any of the

3

Kennedy brothers has experienced. What makes it worse is that only a few months earlier he was on a high arc, heartened by his rising polls, cheered on by the Kennedy faithful and by new voters who had never seen or heard his brothers but were eager to touch history by touching him.

Now much of the glamour has rubbed away with the success. As the little group around the TV set watch him, images about Ted and the family flash through their minds, taken from the media and culture—the wealth of the father, the swift rise of the sons to power, the death in war of one, the public killing of another and another, the swirling controversies over who did the killings, the loyalty of the family clan, the public magic of Jack and Jackie, the family help on making Ted a Senator, a girl drowning in the pond at Chappaquiddick, a TV speech to explain it, his attractive wife living separately from him, his strongly liberal record as Senator, his hard drinking and fast driving, the gossip about women in his life, the "draft" movements he resisted in past presidential elections, his swift rise and abrupt fall in his current candidacy, the specter of his own danger if a nameless someone takes it into his head to shoot, the peril and the glamour and the glory—and again the girl drowning in the pond.

The images that have solidified around Ted have become stereotypes that destroy more than they reveal. His political fortunes have careened wildly. In March 1969, at the start of Richard Nixon's first term, the straw polls showed Ted to be the choice of three out of four Democrats for the 1972 nomination. Four months later, after Chappaquiddick, he wasn't sure he could retain his Senate seat. Ten years later, all through the spring and summer of 1979, there was a poll gap between Ted and President Jimmy Carter wide enough to drive a nomination through, yet soon after Ted announced his candidacy in November his standing plunged disastrously.

What are the operative forces in this tumultuous life? Why the sense of high and tragic destiny attending him? What is responsible for his vulnerable character and erratic conduct? It is a story full of contradictions and surprises.

We start it where it has to start—with the beginnings of an extraordinary immigrant family.

— 2 —

THERE IS no parallel, in the history of the American Presidency, to the closeness and fierce complicity of the Kennedy family. It was a family that moved in three generations from the Irish potato famine and the steerage crossings in packed, disease-infected boats, to a commanding position as America's political aristocracy. Other families have had mobility and success but this one moved faster and more purposively. It took some doing. No wonder its critics call it bitingly an "instant dynasty."

We are all of us products of the great waves of history, "all immigrants," as Franklin Roosevelt said. Edward Moore Kennedy—"Ted" or "Teddy" to follower, opponent, and historian alike—was launched on his senatorial career and his presidential bid by the pressures in the Ireland of the mid-1840's. They sent his great-grandfather, Patrick Joseph Kennedy, along with thousands of others, across the ocean, whether for survival or self-betterment or both. The later wave of the 1880's Irish immigration turned the Kennedys into politicians by providing the succession of brothers with a ready-made ethnic constituency without which they could not hold sway in their little kingdoms.

Like his brothers before him, Ted Kennedy cannot be understood except within these driving family origins which shaped him, gave him political vocation, and propelled him into the stratosphere of American politics.

The family in its "prehistory," before Joe Kennedy refashioned it as his work of art, was modest enough. Patrick Joseph Kennedy, Ted's great-grandfather, was scarcely distinguishable from the rest of those who fled starvation, survived the ocean crossing, and settled on Noodle's Island. Penniless, powerless, and frightened, many had neither the means nor energy to move far from where the boat deposited them. Like the others, Patrick was first a day laborer. But he had some skills and became a cooper, a barrel-maker, on the edges of the liquor industry, giving his son and namesake Patrick the impulsion to move farther up the ladder.

The next in the succession, Patrick Joseph Kennedy, ("P.J."), had more substance and ambition than his father. As tavern keeper (and later as wholesale liquor dealer) he was at the very center of Irish life in America, dispensing advice and help as well as spirits to the Irish countrymen who huddled together in South Boston, as they had once huddled in the steerage of their rat-infested boats.

The genes, or perhaps the expanding opportunities, seemed to improve with the generations. Although the first Patrick Kennedy was hard-working but limited, the second, P.J., was an impressive man who not only ran a good saloon but could be relied on to deliver the vote, distribute patronage, give and receive orders in the feudal hierarchy of the local Democratic Party, and look out for the interests of his constituents as carefully as the local priests looked out for the souls of their parishioners.

What the early Kennedys had in common with other Boston Irish immigrants was the memory of past hardship and injustice in the old country, with its bare subsistence living, its backbreaking toil and absentee landlords, its "Castle Rackrents," its imposed illiteracy qualified only by the "secret schoolmasters" who could evade English scrutiny. They had also in common the central myth of immigrants to America—their feeling that on this continent life would be better tomorrow for their children than it was yesterday for them.

But the special rootedness of the Kennedys lay less in their Irish prehistory than in their history as Americans on the rise, in the two-religion, success-and-achievement-dominated culture of Boston. The life of the Irish in America centered around kinship, conviviality, politics, and religion. The home was the web, religion the rock, the tavern the club, and ward and city politics the dynamic of the Irish immigrants.

They took all four very seriously, begetting and raising children, drinking, politicking, going to mass. The subculture that they spun out of themselves was a dense and cohesive one. It tied them together, giving them a "we-and-they" sense of defending their fortress against adversaries.

— 3 —

TED had the advantage of having two colorful and very different grandfathers as early models. John F. "Honey" Fitzgerald was a prime example of the upwardly mobile Boston Irish. He was the third of seven sons whose mother died when he was sixteen. He moved into the parent vacuum, taking effective charge of those below him, "from teenagers to toddlers," as his daughter Rose put it in her memoir. By his own account he "cooked, made beds, washed the faces of older and younger brothers equally until all of them were men on the streets." He hustled and scraped, and clawed his way up the political ladder to become mayor.

He also moved up the social ladder in Boston Catholic society, although, unlike his son-in-law, he never broke through the wall of separation between the two Bostons—nor did he especially want to. His eccentricities were contained within the mold of his ethnic community. He had a good deal of the buffoon about him, theatrical in everything, tireless in politicking during the day and socializing with political intent every evening.

The two grandfathers expressed two sides of the Irish personality in America—P.J. its solid, closemouthed Catholic puritanism, with rigid values and strict boundaries; Honey Fitz its dervishlike energy, its drive, wit, and charm, and a grandiosity that refused to accept limits.

As a small boy Ted was cherished by both. The personality gulf between the two men persisted into their later years. Honey Fitz delighted in the boy and squired him around Boston, whose every haunt he knew so well. P.J. Kennedy was less effusive, although equally affectionate. The rigor of his code stuck in the minds of the brothers: When they visited their Kennedy grandparents on Sunday afternoons they were not allowed to wink in P.J.'s presence.

Measured by any standard, both P.J. and Honey Fitz were successes. Each had a pride in his Irishness, each made a marriage a little beyond his own social station, each was ambitious for his children. Honey Fitz drew a line between his inviolate family at home, whom he scarcely saw except on weekends, and the public constituency that absorbed his entire day and evening with speeches, christenings, funerals, and political rallies. His wife, Mary Hannon, accepted his absences from home with both tolerance and dignity, a trait she passed on to her daughter Rose.

As it turned out, despite their affectionate scorn for him, the Kennedy boys were to come closer to this model of absentee husband-father and vigorous campaigner than to P.J.'s model of devotion to hearth and home. Ted especially, in his energy and ebullience, felt closer to Honey Fitz, and never tired of convulsing an audience of family and friends by mimicking his oratorical flourishes, with a mocking affection which could not hide the distance the family had traveled from him.

— 4 —

ROOTED as the Kennedy family was, it was also the product of Joseph Kennedy's uninhibited mind and will. His fierce, single-minded purposiveness has been noted in everything written about him. He was a driven man as well as a driving one, spurring himself to achieve his vaulting goals. We tend to forget that, before he turned his energy to finding ways of elevating his sons to the Presidency, he had already conceived of the Kennedy family as a conscious work of art.

He aimed at the start at becoming the progenitor not only of a successful family but of a new aristocracy. It was to be an aristocracy not of manners and sensibility but of power and social position. As we shall see, the energy for it came out of his festering sense of having been somehow cheated, subtly or directly, of his just due in social status by the anti-Catholic exclusionary bigotry of the Boston Brahmin families.

Whatever his true motivations, there is little question that Joe Kennedy saw himself as triumphing over a hostile society. His wizardry consisted of facing what he felt to be a stacked deck and, like an obsessive gambler, contriving a system to beat the game.

The family of five daughters and four sons that he and Rose Fitzgerald brought into the world was rooted in their joint Irish-American heritage. If the parents focused on the sons and pushed the daughters into the background, that too was part of the patriarchal Irish tradition, originating in the land-hunger and masculinism of the Irish peasants.

Yet the family was also an entity that together Joe and Rose invented. He grew hungry for recognition of the sort and on a scale he had not achieved in money-making alone. He communicated to his children, especially to his sons, his conviction that there was nothing beyond their reach, if they would only stretch themselves to grasp it.

These ambitions came only in part out of the family heritage. Kennedy derived much from the very culture that aroused his anger—the traditional Puritan culture of Boston. Writing about the New England of 1800, Henry Adams saw an "oligarchy" ruling it, made up of clergy, lawyers, magistrates, and "respectable society." These elites were structured in families locked together by an endogamy of marriage ties, by education, class, and family. The institutions they created were the church, college, town, and Commonwealth. Adams saw them as "ambitious beyond reason to excel"—a phrase clearly applicable to the Kennedys who came more than a century after them.

Thus in the process of creating themselves as a unique family, the Kennedys both carried over much from their ethnic past and fused it with much from the culture they challenged. To get the other side of the relationship one turns to the *Education of Henry Adams,* with his bitterness over the influx of Irish immigration—and of Italians and Slavs and Jews—who had swamped the old Protestant families by sheer numbers, corrupted his Eden, and brought in the tavern, mass, and ward politics.

—— 5 ——

TO grasp the historic role of the Kennedys, from the original immigrant-progenitors to Edward Moore Kennedy, we must note three developments in the history of Massachusetts. A century and a half after the original great Massachusetts families—Adams, Cabot, Peabody, Lowell—the genetic strain had thinned out, both in business and government, and had become too weak to fight off attacks by the newcomers. This left a vacuum for challengers like the Kennedys to move into.

A second was that these challengers abandoned their own ethnic stockade to advance upon their adversaries. They moved into Boston Latin School and Choate and Milton and Harvard, the citadels of intellectual excellence for the core culture, adopting them as their own. Joe Kennedy operated on the principle that what was best for his opponents was not too good for him. Like his mother before him, who had favored his entering Boston Latin School with its high standards, he wanted to make sure that his sons would move easily among cultivated men.

A third development had to do with public service. Before the Kennedys the ambitions of Irish politicians in America had been local and had stopped with the State and Congressional level. Joseph Kennedy dared—in his plans as well as his dreams—to burst through the barrier and to imagine and will a Kennedy as the first Catholic President.

This was a break with the limitations of ward politics, which had been accepted so long in the Irish subculture. It was a liberating and imaginative break, wedding the adeptness of the Irish at ward level tactics to the high stakes they had not dared risk. Under the spur of the power-hungry newcomers Henry Adams' "ambition beyond reason to excel" became Joe Kennedy's injunction to his sons never to accept second place.

It was in this sense that Joe Kennedy invented the Kennedy dynasty and his sons lived out the Kennedy legend.

2

Joseph Kennedy's Grand Design

— 1 —

T HERE was no time in Ted Kennedy's life, from his birth until Joe Kennedy's stroke, when his father wasn't a power, and from his perspective an omnipotent one. If the material on Ted's grandfather and great-grandfather is skimpy there is a mountain of literature on Joseph P. Kennedy—financier, promoter, philanthropist, the first chairman of the Securities and Exchange Commission, Ambassador to Great Britain, the progenitor of a political dynasty. He was always aware of media power, and invited the mountain to come to him, and when it didn't then he—with his knowledge that in business and politics everything is built on the public image—came to the media mountain. In fact the Kennedy myth began with a number of newspaper and magazine articles he inspired and arranged for.

Born September 6, 1888, an only surviving son among four children, the symbol of his family's upward mobility, Joe was from the start (as often happens in an immigrant culture) a mediator between his family and the larger non-Catholic culture of Boston. But he was also a stepping-stone between the ward heeler Kennedys and the presidential Kennedys.

After his elementary years at Assumption Parochial School, his mother insisted on his going on to non-Catholic schools, Boston Latin School and Harvard ("that place across the river").

Even then he was an operator rather than a good student. He loved Boston Latin but found its scholastic standards pretty exacting, and had to spend an extra year to get through. Yet in every other respect he was a success—handsome, vibrant, with an irresistible persuasiveness and a talent for organizing and for turning a profit on whatever he touched. He was captain of the baseball team, class president, and a universal Pooh-Bah among his fellow students.

At Harvard, where he was again a middling student, but considerably less happy and less a leader than at Boston Latin, he did well enough at sports but excelled in bravado. He conveyed to the other students the image of someone who could tackle and resolve any problem and would some day be heard from. The early *persona* he presented suggested something of the impact the mature man would have on his world.

His character was apparently already formed. He knew what he wanted and the price he was prepared to pay. There was a hint, in the steely eyes and the transfixing gaze, of the cold assessment of reality and the determined will that would brook no resistance to whatever his purpose might be. There are few intimations of the crises of confidence or conscience that mark many life histories in late adolescence and early manhood. If there were any dark broodings or conflicts about his career, he didn't communicate them.

His dream was clearly the traditional American dream of achievement, conquest, and success. He was twelve at the turn of the century, and twenty-three when he graduated from Harvard in 1912. It was a time when social Darwinism was part of the pervasive climate of ideas and values, and without being an intellectual (his favorite boyhood authors were Mark Twain and Horatio Alger) Joe Kennedy was attuned to whatever dominated the atmosphere.

An import from England, social Darwinism fast took on an American coloration, and became a vision of life as a jungle of wills, strivings, and appetites, in which only those survived who were fit for the struggle. To be sure William James, who had already finished his teaching at Harvard before Joe got there, had railed at the "Bitch-goddess Success." But the version of James's "pragmatism" that probably filtered down to Joe, and which he took to heart, was in the cruder form—that the operative truth was whatever worked.

"How can we make some money?" was Joe's usual greeting to his school cohorts. He wanted to make money fast, and moved directly into finance, tested the water, and found it his medium. He served a brief spell as State Assistant Bank Examiner, which gave him a chance to discover who the men were that really counted in life. ("If you're going to get money you have to find out where it is," he said, anticipating Willie Sutton by some decades). Later, on the spoor of the money, he borrowed $45,000, bought control of Columbia Trust, where he had worked for some months and where his father had influence, and at twenty-five became the youngest bank president in the U.S. He had his start, and there was no stopping him.

— 2 —

MEANWHILE he courted Rose Fitzgerald, the mayor's daughter and the belle of Irish Catholic Boston, easily the most glowing and desirable marriage prospect for someone who meant to go as far as Joe did. Since their fathers were important figures in the Boston Irish community, the two young people had often met socially, at dancing, skating, and beach parties.

Rose was the youngest and voted the prettiest girl in her high school graduating class. She was bright, accomplished, traveled. She had been to a convent school in Germany, spoke French, played the piano. Back home she attended the Manhattanville College of the Sacred Heart, and taught Sunday School classes where she encouraged her students to enter religious quiz contests. Her coming-out had been the big event of the year in her world and Joe's.

Rose was her father's treasure. She was the first child and first girl in a brood of six children. Her father thought her a "miracle" —"an impression [she later wrote] from which he never really recovered." While her mother guarded the home fortress Rose was her father's political hostess, accompanying him on his daily royal progress from one civic function to another, and entertaining his important visitors.

Neither of the two families felt overjoyed at first about the match. The Fitzgeralds thought that a mayor's daughter could do better in terms of money and prospects. The Kennedys had dark views about Honey Fitz: P.J. called him "an insufferable clown," and the son-in-law was later to tell Franklin Roosevelt, speaking of one of the Fitzgeralds, "I can't help it if I married into an S.O.B. of a family." For a brief time the slightly star-crossed lovers had to meet secretly, at a variety of rendezvous.

In the end Rose chose Joe from a number of more affluent and promising suitors—the most important conquest he was ever to make—and he later said that for him there was never anyone else. For the nation it was to prove a historic match, even though the marriage later had its rough and stormy passages. For it served as a yeasty mix, and produced the band of brothers and sisters whose impact America was to feel from the mid-forties into the eighties and beyond.

Large families were frequent among Boston's Irish. Rose and Joe Kennedy were agreed on building a family and a home, and on how to bring up the children. There was a generative drive in him that was closely linked with his drive to be best at everything. He went to the limits of whatever he attempted, and building a family was no different from amassing a fortune or gaining power.

There was one difference between his wish for a large family and his other goals. In his business activities Kennedy was less a producer than a juggler and accumulator. He was not a captain of industry in the sense of the inventors and manufacturers who added to the national product. Whether in banking, stocks, underwriting, films, real estate, or liquor distribution, his interest was not in the thing in itself but in money-making. Thorstein Veblen, writing his seminal books during the period of Kennedy's early business ventures, might have used him to illustrate his basic theme on the distinction between "industry" and "finance," between "making goods" and "making money."

But with their family-building Joe and Rose Kennedy were caught up in the thing itself—the wonderfully productive and creative process of making children and a home. It was, for Joe at least, the only aspect of his life that was not primarily a matter of tactic and technique, as business and finance were, and politics and power. His family had a special niche in his life, separate from the sweat and strife of his daily manipulations, the one thing that gave meaning to the rest. He was often to use it as the touchstone by which he tested the worth of decisions on policy—its consequence for the lives and future of his children.

— 3 —

THIS strong sense of family didn't prevent Joe Kennedy from exploring his sexuality beyond it. Except for his refusal to drink or smoke, Kennedy had little of the Puritan in him. He was no small-town Midwestern son of an Evangelical minister, like many captains of industry who scrimped and scrounged to save enough for an education, and then built an empire on the foundation of frugality and saving. On a smaller scale he was more like J. P. Morgan than John D. Rockefeller, more the magnifico than the Puritan.

He took another trait from the Morgan model: the attraction to glamorous women, especially to actresses. And there was nothing covert about his affairs. There was a period of considerable strain in the marriage, when Kennedy sat night after night in fashionable restaurants or nightclubs with a currently successful model or talked-about actress, while Rose was at home with the children. He appeared almost flamboyant on these occasions, sitting at a commanding table, basking in attention, as if to show that no field of conquest was beyond his reach, and that even of the stolen pleasures he claimed only the best.

His California adventure, with Gloria Swanson, was known by their friends and contemporaries, but has been scanted even in the fullest of the biographies. Yet it sheds considerable light on the life-style of a father who was the prime model for his sons. It happened during Kennedy's financial fling at corporate reorganization in Hollywood, and was in part a business relationship, since Kennedy knew a valuable property when he saw one, and was not above fusing business and sentiment.

Gloria Swanson was the current reigning queen of films, an international star, with beauty, glamour and style. Joe organized a production company for her and produced several of her pictures—with losses which the lady ruefully had to make good. But the erotic relationship was more than a flirtation. While there seems to have been no truth in the much bruited story that Miss Swanson's adopted son was named Joseph after Kennedy, or that he was actually Joe's natural child, the relationship was close and strong for a time.

These public demonstrations of dalliance could only have been galling to Rose, who bore them with the outward calm and inner stoicism that became her characteristic response to personal stress. A double standard was traditional in Catholic families, where the husband was accorded special privileges and the wife's concern was for the continuity of the marriage and the stability of the home. The moral for the Kennedy children, especially for the sons, was a clear one, and there is ample evidence that they took it to heart.

Kennedy was restless on every level. As he grew richer he moved his family—after the pattern set by his own parents—to better residential areas. He abandoned the social frustrations of Boston to move to the New York area, where, unlike in Boston, his wife and daughters could belong to the good social clubs. He found a winter residence in Palm Beach and a summer one in Hyannisport, to which the children returned from their schools, colleges, travels, adventures, and around which the family rituals and lore clustered.

He was a figure out of Theodore Dreiser, who had anticipated him in his portrait of Frank Cowperwood in *The Titan* and *The Financier,* with his fusion of money, power, and eros. Dreiser, himself from a strict Catholic family in Indiana, trying to rid himself of the Puritan overlay of guilt, saw his hero as a "varietist." Joseph Kennedy, a pluralist in everything, including his sexual life, was a prime instance of this emerging omnivorous character type.

He lived in a plurality of homes, pursued his money ventures in a plurality of fields (banking, stocks, real estate holdings, corporate reorganizations, films, oil), had a plurality of children and a plurality of extramarital attachments. He was freewheeling in his business methods, tied down to no single industry, area, residence, or office, transacting his business by a telephone network to trusted lieutenants who were like an extension of himself. He was a freebooter, mocking the financial establishment, pirating whatever treasure came to view. He was able to see fresh juxtapositions, bring incompatible worlds together, and do easily what others found hard or impossible.

He saw and taught his sons to see possibilities in every situation that others overlooked. He encouraged them to slit through the mask of convention, rhetoric, and hypocrisy ("forget the rhetoric," "cut the crap," "no Kennedy shits himself") to get at the "bottom line"—the residual nexus of reality and control at which money, politics and power meet.

— 4 —

TED'S birth in 1932—a "surprise" gift, a kind of bonus baby—came at the prime of life for his parents (Joe at forty-four, Rose at thirty-nine), bringing the family child census to nine.

It came also at a turning point in Joe's life, when he was moving from local financing (Boston, then Hollywood) to the national stage, and from a purely business involvement to a political one as well. For 1932 was the year of Franklin Roosevelt's first presidential campaign, and all of Joe's later presidential politics for himself and for his sons derived in one way or another from his relation to Roosevelt.

Franklin D. Roosevelt became successively Kennedy's ideal and model, his boss, his antagonist, his nemesis. He was one of the few men Kennedy could not outwit, the only man in his life who charmed, obsessed, fascinated, frustrated, and finally outfoxed him. Yet after Roosevelt's death the political lessons Kennedy had learned from him became the stuff of a new life purpose. He could say, with Nietzsche, "What does not destroy me strengthens me."

Up to his Roosevelt experience Kennedy swam in the sea of finance, where he showed himself swift, strong, and expert. With Roosevelt he moved to the field of political policy and tactic. He proved good at the tactic, wretched at policy—which was what undid him.

It was from his relationship with Roosevelt that Kennedy got the idea of the Presidency as a personal possibility. FDR was both a hero for him and a model for instruction. If Roosevelt could do it, why not he?

It oversimplifies to say, as some psycho-historians have done, that Kennedy used his sons as leverage for assuaging his own early social hurt, and that getting the Presidency for them was a way of striking back in revenge. The fact is that he wanted the Presidency for himself before he thought of it for his sons. And he wanted it not just as revenge but as a power base. Economic power was all very well, but political power at the summit level could beat it any day, because it led to every other power form.

When he encountered Roosevelt he knew he had a comer, and he passed the word on to his business associates, who were still under the spell of Herbert Hoover's free enterprise fixation. "Jot down the name of the next President," he told a business friend. "It's Franklin D. Roosevelt. And don't forget who told you."

Some six months after Ted's birth, Joe Kennedy worked a miracle at the Democratic Convention, when FDR faced the loss of the nomination unless he could win over John Nance Garner's Texas delegation. The key to Garner was William Randolph Hearst, and Kennedy managed to persuade his good friend Hearst that Roosevelt wouldn't bring the end of the world. During the campaign the man who had conquered a half-dozen fields of finance found himself a relatively minor if also mysterious figure on the Roosevelt train, lining up business support for him.

After the election he waited for his reward with growing impatience and hurt, while Roosevelt's inner circle of advisers leisurely debated what, if anything, he should be given. In the end he was made chairman of the newly created Securities and Exchange Commission. It was a case, as many at the time (including this writer) wryly noted, of getting the marauder to tend the sheep. But FDR countered that Kennedy, from his piratical experience on Wall Street, would at least know how the stealing was done, and Kennedy was resolved (in his own words) to acquit himself well for the sake of his brood.

It worked out well, and Joe Kennedy, the freebooter of Wall Street, did a sturdy job of guarding the flock, and resigned when he had given the Commission a good start. Many among the unbelievers who had cried havoc had to eat their words. Kennedy was building a record for himself, to be used for political advancement when the time came. The post he coveted was the Treasury. FDR gave it in succession to William Woodin and Henry Morgenthau, two close friends who would cause him no policy headaches. Kennedy was a prima donna. "The trouble with Kennedy is that you always have to hold his hand," said FDR.

Kennedy waited, with hope and heartbreak alternating within him. By the time of the second campaign, in 1936, FDR had moved sharply left, but Kennedy stood fast and wrote a campaign book—*I'm for Roosevelt.* He swallowed even FDR's Supreme Court packing plan, waited impatiently again for the promised reward. It finally came, to Kennedy's delight: the ambassadorship to London.

— 5 —

IT was an outrageous appointment and showed at once Roosevelt's willfulness and his wild miscalculation of Kennedy's mind and priorities. He told intimates that Kennedy was "too dangerous to have around" and that he had therefore sent him out of the country—but that was exactly where the dark shadow of the future loomed. One suspects that Roosevelt got a roguish pleasure from sending an Irish ward heeler's son and a reformed Wall Street wolf to the Court of St. James—the in-joke of the week for FDR and his intimates.

But it was no joke for the British nor for Kennedy himself. Somehow he made the Himalayan blunder of convincing himself that isolationism was the wave of the future, and he found his wretched cause in a continuous lobbying for the appeasement of Hitler.

One can describe what ingredients went into this recipe for self-destruction: the heady flattery of the Cliveden set in England, his fears of what a devastating war would do to his fortune, and, deepest of all, his premonitions (which proved alas all too true) about the fate of the children he had given as hostages to fortune. There was also his bottom-line sense that the Nazis had the guns and planes to clobber Europe, that the United States would be a patsy to try to save it, and that the best hope lay in a fortress America saving itself and surviving during a long bleak period of Nazi domination.

There was doubtless the added hunch, since he expected Roosevelt to leave after two terms, that an anti-war record as Ambassador to London, along with his achievements in finance and government and his strong family image, would make him acceptable as a likelier successor to FDR than anyone on the horizon.

Whatever his motives, his calculation went wrong. After a brief honeymoon he managed to alienate the British, especially after the Chamberlain government itself discovered that Munich didn't work and that Hitler was unappeasable. Roosevelt had read the auguries, and after his *cordon sanitaire* speech in 1937 he knew that America would have to throw its weight into the balance to restore the world power equilibrium.

We now know how tortuous was the path FDR took toward his objective of containing the spread of Nazi domination. With his strong Catholic and business ties, Kennedy was almost as important to Roosevelt as the President was to him. Kennedy felt baffled but was too blindly lost in his anti-war cause to grasp the subtlety in Administration policy.

When he did finally register FDR's sustained purpose he assigned it to the influence of the Jews and the pro-British press. FDR in turn was enraged at his busybody ambassador ("he's a pain in the neck to me"), and he and the State Department bypassed him in negotiating with the British until Kennedy was climbing the wall in frustration and rage.

The final blow came when Kennedy learned that Roosevelt had no intention of surrendering the ship of state in 1940, exactly when he felt he was needed most at the helm. Kennedy had already sent up some smoke signals, through trusted lieutenants in the media and the party, suggesting that he was Presidential material, even if not *papabile*. But with Roosevelt more and more like the banyan tree, in whose shade no one else could grow, the Kennedy boomlet came to nothing.

The lonely ambassador waited again, eating his heart out in London, but no signal reached him from the wily President who now saw him as a potential enemy and wanted no open break. Desperate, Kennedy announced he was coming home. He was in close touch with Henry Luce, of *Time,* and there was dark talk and an apparently well-founded expectation that he would declare for Wendell Willkie.

He arrived ten days before the election, pursued by telegrams from Roosevelt commanding him to keep silent until he had talked with the President. At a family dinner that night at the White House, Roosevelt, with the help of Joe's friend James F. Byrnes, got out of Kennedy the promise of support he wanted. Perhaps Kennedy—as his son Jack recounted it—got from Roosevelt in return a vague intimation of support for the Presidency in 1944. Possibly Roosevelt—as his son James believed—hinted darkly at making the political life of the Kennedy sons difficult if their father turned Judas. With his combination of threat and guile, Roosevelt wheedled out of the reluctant but bedazzled ambassador the promise of his badly needed endorsement for a third term. Roosevelt was no king of righteousness, nor was Joe Kennedy exactly a searcher after the Holy Grail of principle. They reached some accommodation perforce. Kennedy fulfilled his promise in a half-hour radio talk that may indeed have reassured the marginal conservatives.

But once reelected, Roosevelt moved on to entangle American opinion in his sustained effort to develop an allied counterforce to Nazi power in Europe. After the "phony war" phase, with Hitler's air blitz on England, Kennedy's situation as ambassador grew ever more isolated. Churchill and Roosevelt both ignored him. He returned to America and gave a disastrous interview to Louis Lyons of the Boston *Globe* that left the nation aghast with its crude expression of his sloppy thinking on the war, the British, the Nazis, and the Jews. He never lived it down, and it haunted all three sons in their campaigns.

—— 6 ——

THEY were a discordant pair, these two. Their careers converged, but they themselves never really connected with each other. Each man tried to use the other, and it was Roosevelt who came away with the advantage. Once he had squeezed Kennedy dry he threw the husk away.

Kennedy was clearly out of his element in foreign policy, and beyond his depth in tangling with Roosevelt, intellectually and temperamentally. FDR was as invulnerable to Kennedy's bluster as he was to his charm. Kennedy never lost a haunting sense that the patrician of Hyde Park, who jollied and toyed with him, never accepted him as an intellectual or social equal. FDR was amused by Kennedy, played at "educating" him, and enjoyed some of his back-room language and stories. But mostly he saw him as a know-how man, a mercenary who never had a true feeling for the New Deal nor a coherent philosophy.

I have explored the relations of the two men because, by a curious irony, the chastening experience Joe had with FDR made him more determined to found a political dynasty. If this was what power could do, for its wielder, and to its victim, then you had better get hold of it.

His life was split in two. Up to his mid-forties, in 1932, he was the jaunty amasser and possessor of a fortune, a hardheaded realist concerned with means and tactics only, leaving public policy to others. If he had remained that man, there would never have been a Kennedy dynasty nor three presidential campaigns by his three sons.

Then he found that his hope for the Presidency was not to be. He must have sensed it earlier, but he knew it for sure in the fall of 1940, when he was trapped into the third-term endorsement.

After the London blitz he returned to Boston and Hyannisport, to his old base of operations. His focus was still on the Presidency, but from now forward no longer for himself but for his children.

3

Patriarch, Great Mother, Band of Brothers

— 1 —

BECAUSE so much happened to the Kennedys so publicly we see in them not only their own individual life histories but the repetitive patterns that are generic to us all, much as the audiences at Greek tragedies saw in the House of Atreus what was generic to them.

Every family is a polity—a political entity—with relations of authority, power, rights, responsibilities. It is also an emotional and psychological constellation, with relations of love and hate, affection and alienation, security and insecurity. As each new member enters or leaves the family, the relations shift, as they do when crucial events change, either the parental pair-bond or the individual family members.

Joe Kennedy was not a domineering but a dominant father, whose action and authority flowed to every family member. He was always voluble, a teller of tales, a bringer of news and visitors from the world outside. He presented himself in a succession of roles—the Young Banker, the Financier, the Commissioner, the Patriarch—and finally the name that stuck when the role had vanished, the ambassador. He was not a harsh father—in fact, a surprisingly gentle one, especially with Ted, and often supportive to the children in crisis. But in the crunch it was his authority they had to reckon with. No child of such a father could fail to be imprinted by this strong male model.

—— 2 ——

ROSE Kennedy was, in archetypal terms, the Great Mother. No one could doubt either her strength or her spirited intelligence. And she played the mother role to the hilt.

The Grand Design for the boys, as they grew older, was left to the father, but the daily execution was Rose Kennedy's province. She fulfilled it with relish and a high sense of duty. Whatever the hurts Joe Kennedy inflicted on her, she never questioned his authority as father. She transmitted even the minutiae of his authority to the children: his rules for the breakfast and dinner table, the need to be quiet during his afternoon naps.

During the earlier years of the marriage, when Joe's absences were frequent, Rose ran the family and brought up the children by principles they had both agreed on. Their understanding was that Rose would be the dominant determiner of rules for the children in the early years, but even then her authority was clearly surrogate for his.

She had organized everything in her life and nothing escaped her attention. Running a family with nine children and with homes and apartments scattered everywhere, Rose became managerial. She kept an index-card file on her children and peppered them with memos on the tiniest details. She was—as her son Jack was later to say—the "glue that held the family together." She was a compulsive world traveler and sightseer, took her children on the round of churches, galleries, and ruins, and used Joe's acquaintanceship with famous people as a means of educating the children about the larger world.

Life with such a parent was one long pedagogical excursion. Her appearance was deceptive: she was petite, beautiful, skilled in feminine accomplishments, the darling of the Parisian couturiers. Yet she could converse with heads of state, make a speech, hold a "Boston Tea Party" for a campaigning son. She had grace, charm, beauty, verve, style—and a psyche with the tensile strength of steel.

From his birth Ted lived in a household dominated by politics. When he was five his father became an important part of the New Deal, riding herd on the stock market, policing the issuing of securities, involved with the jockeying for position and the clash of policies. This determined the family conversation among the grown-ups and the older children. The father didn't like any talk of money or money-making at the table. He made it clear that the boys were meant for higher things, which meant politics.

Ted was weaned on politics. His lullabies, his mother said, were political lullabies. His father brought political people home to dinner, directed political questions at Joe Jr. and Jack in a kind of catechism that the youngest could only register as something serious. Later came London and the embassy, and the excitement of the air raids. On the family's return the talk was of war or not-war, and then of the enlistment of the two oldest brothers. By the war's end Ted was entering his teens and the talk, dark and tragic now, was starting to mean something.

—— **3** ——

FOR an insight into the Kennedy family structure and its effects on the youngest as well as the older children, one must start with the idea of kinship, kingship and patriarchy. The Kennedy family was a polity ruled by a king, backed always by an eldest son, on the principle that the inheritance passes through him.

The sense of family kinship was close, even clannish. But the line of authority was clear: It was from the father, augmented or mediated by the queen-consort or the heir-presumptive who, as the children grew older, was the king's surrogate, meting out a ready if dubious justice in his absence.

In sheer financial terms, by reason of tax laws as well as sound parenting, Joe Kennedy saw to it that trust funds were established early and equally for each of the children. When his friend Hearst noted scornfully that this would give them the independence to leave, Joe shot back, "If my kids leave I would be a lousy father." But in terms of the family seen as polity, what ate into the consciousness of the children—and into the threshold below the conscious—was the constant reminder that the power emanated from the father-king, whoever his surrogate might be.

He might use his authority with a severe directness, as little Ted learned when he ventured home from school alone, against orders, and got a coat hanger's ministrations on his backside. But this was rare. More often the patriarch kept order by voice and words and eyes. There was the dreaded sharpness in his tone when he ended one of Jack's needling comments with "We won't talk about that anymore," or when he addressed an over-conscientious but exhausted Bobby with "Why aren't you back in Washington on your job?" And the imperious voice was backed up by the all-seeing Cyclopean eye.

As a patriarchal family, in the Old Testament sense, the Kennedys clung to the idea of the first-born as the chosen vessel for transmitting the family's strength. This was clearly the way the father-king, and the rest, felt about Joe Jr. as the heir-presumptive. Not only was he most like his father, in looks, physique, command, but he was in addition everything his father had wanted to be. He was the shining prince, with excellent college grades, articulate, a leader among his peers, devastating with girls. The second brother by comparison was left in the shadows, the third thrown for years into gloomy fits of inner struggle.

— 4 —

WE turn to the Greek idea of *agon,* the wrestling with others and self for excellence. Like the Greeks, Joe and Rose Kennedy didn't recognize second best in any contest. To come in second was to lose. To grow up a Kennedy was in this literal sense *agonizing—*

a continuous process of struggle, within and outside the family.

It didn't operate scholastically, in school and college grades, because the Kennedy values system was not primarily intellectual, and because the experience of the father had been that you can win in the essential life contests with indifferent grades.

What counted in *agon* were the home and family sports: boat-racing, touch football, roughhouse. Given the unspoken but clearly communicated intra-family struggles over recognition, self-esteem, authority, one can understand the psychic intensity that went into these contests and the symbolic meaning they carried, later extended to other and greater battles.

One can understand also the emergence of the Kennedy family style—the rough black humor, the corrosive irony, the teasing and self-deprecating twist of phrase, the characteristic fusion of affectionate put-down and disguised hostility. How many old family scores were settled in these *agon* bouts, how many psychic hurts healed or revenged, how many injustices redeemed or intensified!

But outsiders discovered that the score-settling intensity was strictly an intra-family affair: No outsider could intervene. Whatever their competition with each other the brothers—and sisters —closed ranks against the outside world. They could say anything they wanted against each other, but let no outsider say anything against any of them! They had to outrun, outsail, outplay, outdistance, outpummel one another and anyone else within their reach. In fact, when they beat others, it was as Kennedys that they triumphed, as representatives of a family and a clan.

—— 5 ——

THE transition from family contests and adolescent games to the political arena was gradual but inexorable. The whole struggle finally became encoded in the ordeal of politics. No matter what his financial triumphs, Joe Kennedy could never have defined his family and made it dynastic by continuing to make money and carry through corporate reorganizations. Even the Rockefellers and Mellons, after their fortune was amassed, turned to public service. For money is not the civic, constitutive principle that politics is.

The new Joe Kennedy transmitted to his sons his new sense of the need to prepare for the political vocation. Because he wanted Joe Jr. to do what he had himself failed to do, he sent him to law school, envisaged a political career for him, followed each of his feats proudly. When he got the embassy post in London it was doubly precious: along with the personal recognition it opened to the older boys a complex, sophisticated world which, in the British tradition, linked social position with political vocation.

So the older brothers wandered around Europe, and worked at the embassy or as amateur foreign correspondents. Joe Jr. studied at the London School of Economics (Jack had to forego it only because of illness), and even traveled in the Soviet Union with Harold Laski, arguing socialism and capitalism with one of the best academic intelligences on the British Left.

It was an ideal preparation for a career in high politics. When his own dreams of the Presidency ran into the shoals of his quarrel with Roosevelt, Joe Sr.'s grand design for Joe Jr. became an obsession.

From that point on he became a dedicated political craftsman, bent on giving his sons an inheritance, not after his death but during his life, which would enable them to transcend him. Joe Jr. was the ideal chosen vessel to carry out this plan. He had all the qualities of *persona,* mind, leadership, character.

He was also close to his father in his political views: he was anti-war, believed in a fortress America, was critical of the more liberal phases of the New Deal, was tough-minded and contemptuous of liberal rhetoric or wishful idealism.

During the troubled years of Joe Sr. over isolationism, Joe Jr. took positions that went even beyond his father's. In 1940, when the ambassador gave Roosevelt a reluctant endorsement, his son, as a Massachusetts delegate, raised a dissenting voice in the National Convention against the choice of FDR by acclamation.

But the father's Grand Design for his sons was not ideological. Politics as vocation was too important to be deflected by ideological differences. The Kennedys would always be Democrats, but in the Kennedy mind politics assumed a reality in itself, quite aside from the program or society it might envisage. It became in this sense totemic, fox and lion together, and the totem of politics became the signature of the Kennedy clan.

This was the family and social climate in which Ted grew toward his teens, largely unaware of the meaning of the grand events the others discussed. The early 1940's were hard years for the family, with both the older boys away fighting, and the dread war that Joe Kennedy had striven against—and been broken by politically—now a reality.

Yet the ambassador and his wife had somehow struggled through to a new view of themselves, their children, their mission in life. The fortune he amassed was estimated at something like 400 million dollars. But there was a new clarity, and a new hope along with it, that reached beyond the fortune. Chastened by his defeats but armed with hope, the patriarch, and Rose as the Great Mother, awaited the return of their older sons from the war and presided over the rest of their brood, especially the growing pains of Ted, their youngest.

CHAPTER II

SHAPING A KENNEDY

1/The Late-Born

2/Moratorium: Rebelling, Probing Limits, Expiating

3/Finding His Vocation, Winning His Spurs

4/Becoming His Own Man: The Path to the Senate

1

The Late-Born

— 1 —

"THE GREAT heroic deed," wrote Hannah Arendt, "is to be born." And in a Kennedy family—crowded, competitive, demanding—there was daring in being born. But to be born the fourth son and the youngest and final child of nine placed a burden of heroism on the newcomer.

Not in any outward way. He had a warm welcome. He was the prize physical specimen of the family. Everyone delighted in his bubbling energy and his overflowing health, which even today make him a commanding figure of a man and a physical prototype of leadership. For his brothers he was a young cub to lick into shape. For his sisters, who were always held secondary to the boys, he was a thing of wonder, whom they could cosset and pamper to their heart's delight. For his parents he was the unexpected but welcome dividend, the clinching evidence that the family he rounded out was the best investment of their lives.

But growing up youngest, even as a son, in a family that placed such emphasis on birth order, was only a little less hard than growing up as a daughter.

In the Kennedy family, it was hard to be not only the youngest but—here I use James M. Burns's phrase—the "late-born." There was an eighteen-year spread from Ted to Joe Jr., a fifteen-year gap to Jack, and almost an eight-year gap to his nearest brother Bob.

35

The rest of the children were bunched closely enough to compete with each other. For the late-born it was hopeless to compete with his brothers until he had outgrown his chubby years and early teens and caught up with them physically, in late adolescence. It was galling, until then, to be bracketed with the girls or shielded by the parents. In a competitive family the only thing worse than not winning is to be out of the running because you are too young.

In addition to the constant presence of hierarchy there was always a sense of bustle and change, and momentous things happening that you stretched yourself to be part of. One thinks of William James's description of a small child's world as "a great big, buzzing, booming confusion."

Dad was often away, and when at home he was always talking about changes to come, and new jobs to get, and who was ahead of whom in Washington. The older boys were going or coming between schools and home. And Mother and the girls were dressing up for whatever occasions in their own hectic orbit. There were the family trips to Longchamps for lunch and a Radio City film, and there were Dad's offices in Washington and all the men with big cigars, and the press conferences, and the sun and golf carts in Palm Beach, and sailing on a kayak of your own at Hyannisport, and all the succession of schools in whatever cities the family alighted in, like birds perching on a chance bough.

And there was London, and seeing your picture in the English and American papers, and the London bobbies with a name like your brother's, and reporters and photographers always hovering while you peered at their notepads and heard the camera shutters click, and Mother and Kick and Rosemary being presented to the Queen, and Dad wearing striped pants instead of knickers at Court (he said it would have destroyed him in the American papers), and everyone calling him "Your Excellency" ("Is that your new name, Dad?"), and Kick going off for weekends to the dukes and duchesses and helping Mother as hostess, and running the strange elevators in the six-story residence and riding the lorries in Grosvenor Square, and grief over the goldfish that died in your room, and the air-raid wardens and having your own gas mask to put on, and the Paris apartment, and the villa at Antibes with the blue water, and people speaking funny languages, and (in between) coming back for visits to Boston and Washington and Palm Beach, and Dad on the phone talking and laughing but often looking glum and angry.

In the stream of consciousness of a six- or eight- or ten-year-old child, with his own perspectives, big events were often foreshortened and trivial details enlarged. We can only guess at the impact of the booming confusion of the everyday Kennedy world on a little boy with devastating animal energy.

With everything moving so fast there were rituals of order and manners to be imposed, and constant pressures of decorum and performance. In such a setting how could one keep from measuring the distances between self and brothers, and the unmeasurable one between self and father? How could a small boy, even a good one, keep from storing up memories, dreams, hopes, and sometimes resentments? How not explode occasionally, or move to redress the unjust balance that made him always acted upon, never actor and initiator?

Life in those young years was an incalculable flux. Every house they lived in was a movable pageant of activity. True, Hyannisport was to become, on their return from London, a genuine homeplace, a relaxed, accustomed haven. But that was later. The family moved so frequently that by the time Ted got to Milton Academy he had been to ten private schools (Bobby had been to six). It was clearly a family whose orbits swirled around the central figure of the patriarch, and it was not a good way for a boy to get a steady base for friendships, studies, values.

— 2 —

TED'S early years had thus clearly more discontinuities than continuities, more confusions than clarity. His authority figures were at once too flamboyant and distant for a young boy struggling to see himself on a level with his father and brothers. Their feats of language and action must have dazzled him, and while he might feel he could equal them in sailing, football, tennis, he knew that in other skills they were beyond his reach. They were enough older so that their adventures seemed to Ted, in his adolescence, part of another world. William James—as his younger brother Henry put it—was born only fifteen months ahead of him "and I have spent the rest of my life trying to catch up."

The world of the private school, for the sons of the rich, is not as damaging to American boys as its model and counterpart, the British public school, has been to English upper-class boys. Yet Jack was wretched at Groton and warned his brother away. Bob tried a Catholic school, Priory, but left and spent his last two years at Milton, where he was much happier. For Ted, Milton was also a good choice, although he didn't make the abiding friendships in it that Bob did, nor was he at the time as pious as Bob, who tried to convert the school to Catholicism. Ted was less shy, more gregarious, made friends more easily but not as strongly.

His young years had by then been twice touched by tragedy and loss. The first time, when Ted was nine, his oldest sister, Rosemary—a retarded girl astray in a highly competitive family —grew too difficult to manage at home, and had to be sent off at twenty-three to an institution in Wisconsin.

When he was twelve two priests came to the house at Hyannisport where the family was awaiting Young Joe's return from the war, to tell the father that his first-born had been killed in a highly dangerous bombing mission. Grown suddenly old, the father had gone to his room and shut the door.

In the spring of Ted's second year at Milton, tragedy struck a third time, when he got word that his sister Kathleen ("Kick") had died in the crash of a private plane over the Ardeches, in France. He left for home abruptly, before his Congressman brother, Jack, could arrive to take him along to the grieving family. It was a diminished family now, with the six children left —three sons, three daughters—and the desolated parents.

"After the first death there is no other." The Dylan Thomas

line suggests how the first blinding loss may have set the pattern for those to come in its impact on the father. He had to come to grips with a fate stronger than all his designs.

— 3 —

WITH the death of Joe Jr., the chosen carrier of his father's political dream, the next son, Jack, became inevitably the prime inheritor of the family's political fortunes. The father had intended to run Young Joe for a Congressional seat. This goal was now transferred to Jack, who, after some doubts, was galvanized into a new sense of purpose and political vocation by the infusion of his family's confidence in him. He settled into his new role, running as a war hero and with his father's help developing a campaign presence and technique whose effectiveness carried a bright promise for the future Kennedy politics. It served as a declaration by the family against the blind irrationality of Young Joe's death, and at the same time it gave meaning to the death by the closing of family ranks as the second-born moved into the first-born's place.

Young Ted, just entered at Milton, must have registered the transition, although he couldn't know how fateful it was—the first ritual of picking up of the fallen standard, as he would some day himself act out the last. He was at work on his freshman studies that fall of 1946 when Jack campaigned and won his seat, but old enough to be excited by the family's first election victory. At the celebration of Jack's victory the patriarch asked Ted whether he had a toast, and Ted solemnly proposed one to "our brother who is not here." Already he had glimpsed the meaning of change and continuity in the family life.

It was a burden he had to bear, young as the shoulders were that it fell upon. The final impact of being late-born was that while the blows of the family tragedies came to his brothers and sisters when they were old enough to meet them, they came to Ted at a perilously early age, and they left their mark at a time when the young psyche was striving to give order to its universe.

During Ted's Milton years, Bob was mostly away, getting through law school, getting married, starting a family of his own, perhaps as *his* answer to death. It was Jack, now in Congress, who drew closer to Ted, gradually taking Young Joe's place as the surrogate father.

Ted worked hard and reasonably well at his studies, although he needed considerable tutoring. But he found it easier to express himself through sports. He was solid at football, if not as fast and imaginative as Bobby had been. A coach could always rely on him to carry through a play as he was instructed to do, but the added bit of initiative and improvising that makes a good athlete—as it makes a good political tactician—wasn't there.

He did well at debate, could master a subject thoroughly and muster rebuttal arguments. He had a capacity for engaging accommodation to people of every condition, and his older brothers later called him the family's "best politician."

What he was already developing at Milton was the genial, open, but serious *persona:* the face presented to others, to win acceptance and support but also, perhaps indispensably, to hide one's true emotions and sheath one's vulnerability. It is hard to escape the feeling, in these teenage years of Ted, up to eighteen, that a struggle had already begun between the shaping of the public mask and the private face and interiority.

2

Moratorium: Rebelling, Probing Limits, Expiating

— 1 —

WITH HIS entry into Harvard, Ted began a cyclical behavior pattern which was to crop up in a more serious form later in life. It was one of drift and unhappiness, followed by a fugue of irrational action, followed in turn by remorse and an effort at self-redemption.

In any life there are bound to be tragedies and reverses, and their impact on the psyche depends on what phase of the life history they occur in, and what else is happening. All the Kennedy brothers, except perhaps "Young Joe," tended toward a slow maturing. Jack was rescued from his career dawdling and catapulted into early adulthood by the war and—with his brother's death—by the enforced plunge into politics. He proved himself equal to the new pressures and was exhilarated by his testings and his expanding vistas. Bob, younger and by nature gloomier—with black moods—plunged into law school and law practice, and an early start on raising a family of his own, the generativity in him serving in part as a defiance to the deaths. He was also old enough, as Ted was not, to work actively in Jack's election campaigns, and, after an unhappy spell with the McCarthy investigating committee, as counsel for his brother's Senate subcommittee on labor racketeering.

Jack and Bob struck a remarkably effective alliance in working together. Each had traits that reinforced the other's. They knew they were working within the larger design set by their father, but together they also knew how to set limits on his pressures.

Thus the two brothers took the tragedies in their stride, coping with the career demands that stretched their talents to the limit. Ted, old enough to be anxious about his own gifts, too young to use them except in preparing himself for something vaguely ahead, was caught willy-nilly in a marking-time phase of his life. He could neither escape into reality nor use it to fill the void left by the emotional losses. All of this added to his increasing sense of being limited to the essentially unreal world of school and college while his older brothers had already started to fulfill the family mandate.

Ted's moratorium, his period of seeming stasis, came at seventeen or eighteen, somewhat later than to most adolescents. It was made more painful by his sense of being left out. While his brothers were moving surely and swiftly ahead—Jack in Congress, aiming at the Senate, and Bob testing himself as counsel for several investigative congressional committees—nothing was happening to him except school and college.

It was not in general a good time for the college young. The idealism of the war was over, the "beat generation" had moved in, and the apathy of the fifties lay ahead. Ted found friends most easily among the "jocks" and "playboys." As a freshman he chose mostly the "gut" courses, in part out of the prevailing skepticism about the value of academic achievement, in part perhaps out of hostility toward the role assigned to him.

He fitted all too easily into the mocking stance his friends adopted toward a too sober and too achieving adult world. His two older brothers had been war heroes, and he had plenty of physical grit himself. But for the moment the role he chose was a cool one, derisive of the exaggerated sanctities of life. He seems to have been cool about sex too, making no pretenses about romantic love or emotional involvement and making his sexual approaches to attractive girls with a matter-of-fact directness and an absence of personal commitment that sometimes startled them.

— 2 —

THE episode of Ted's use of a stand-in to take his Spanish exam has been variously interpreted as a youthful peccadillo, a rebellion against the too competitive family, and a dark sign of early corruption.

Ted seems to have arranged for another freshman student— known as the "Master of Spanish" for his knowledge of the language—to take the spring final exam for him. Alas, a proctor recognized him when he handed in the exam paper with Kennedy's name on it. The dean was informed, both culprits were swiftly summoned, and both were "severed" from Harvard. They could re-apply as reformed characters, after a year.

A minor episode? Certainly not a saturnalia of wickedness. But it was nonetheless symptomatic of Ted's vagueness of self-perception and his blurred judgment, and a sign that all was not well with him nor with his setting. It was in reality a muddled, impulsive and dim-witted failure of judgment on the part of a still immature young man with considerable identity confusion. This fits best what followed later in life, setting a pattern of confusion, blunder, remorse, expiation, rebuilding, that was to be repeated on a larger canvas.

More formidable for Ted than the dean's action was his father's wrath. The more the patriarch thought of it the madder he got. Here he was, busy with plans for Jack's upcoming bid for the Senate, and here was this damnfool bit of juvenile idiocy.

Joe Kennedy moved swiftly. The story didn't get into the papers for another eleven years, when Ted ran for the Senate. Ted, remorseful, set about redeeming himself. Jack later told how Ted might have turned out a "playboy" if his father had not used "toughness" and cracked down on him. This application of deterrence theory would be more persuasive if both father and Big Brother had not seen it as a problem in naughtiness and discipline, amenable to "toughness." There is no indication that they gave much thought to the turmoils there were in Ted's own mind.

Ted's next move was the classical one for a boy who feels a deep guilt. He enlisted in the Army. And not simply enlisted—he came home to say he had signed up for four years of service in Korea as a PFC. It was a touching gesture by a downcast, vulnerable boy. His two oldest brothers had enlisted in war: Why not he? If they could do it then he could do it too. He would be a man, and on his own terms.

But the patriarch was aghast. ("Boy, don't you ever look at what you're signing?") The war had killed one son and put another in a Navy hospital for months. He wasn't giving a third hostage recklessly. He pulled strings, got the four years reduced to two, and the venue changed after boot camp from Korea to Paris and Germany.

—— 3 ——

FOR Ted, despite the dreariness of two Army years, it turned out to be a good experience. For the first time he was like his brothers, coping with reality—and he was doing it on his own, in his own way. He didn't make a record as a war hero, as Jack and Young Joe did. But he did what he had to, with no prodding from father and brothers. He had started his expiation.

The years from eighteen to twenty-four must be seen as a testing period for Ted, between a late adolescence and a delayed young manhood. In his troubled phase, especially in the Spanish exam episode, he explored the limits of the permissible, and emerged with grief for himself and his family.

His task, during the period as a whole, was to move from

doubt and confusion to self-trust. Whether he did it lastingly will emerge as we follow the rest of his story. He did cope with it, and had the resilience to overcome what might have been a greater damage to his entire college career. The two Army years tested his self-command. The three remaining Harvard years, on his reentry (he was judged to have rehabilitated himself), tested his perseverance and his ability to resume his not always congenial studies and see them through. He set no academic record at Harvard, but the important fact was that he got through.

Both the Army and college experiences showed an aspect of Ted that is sometimes overshadowed by the more dramatic events of his life. With a family like the Kennedys an episode like the Spanish exam was less a moral issue than one involving public consequences. Ted had lost his role as the baby and the family pet, and emerged as a potential problem youth. He had brought grief on his family, especially his father. But he also showed in the sequel that he could accept discipline, meet the demands made on him, and resume with his damaged career line.

3

Finding His Vocation, Winning His Spurs

— 1 —

TIME, SAID Henri Bergson, is not made up of equally paced mathematical units, but has a varying intensity as it slows down or speeds up in the years of our days and the days of our years. The dozen years between eighteen and thirty in Ted Kennedy's life—the true years of coming of age and becoming one's own man—are illumined by Bergson's insight.

They fall roughly into four phases, each of them a three-year period: the troubled years—the disastrous one as a Harvard freshman, the other two on Army assignment; the more stable but still dragging period as Ted settled down doggedly but unhappily to finish at Harvard; the law school years at the University of Virginia, happier and swifter years that included his courtship and marriage, a glowing Moot Court success, and his glimpse of his true vocation; and his last period, moving at a dizzying pace, crowding a young lifetime of new starts and completions as he hurtled from the callow law school graduate to his election, at thirty, as U.S. Senator from Massachusetts.

A detached observer, watching Ted in the first half of this twelve-year stretch, might have wondered whether the youngest Kennedy would ever amount to more than one of those mediocre, failed scions of a rich and powerful family, carried along by inherited wealth, passive and essentially self-indulgent, basking in the

46

family's reflected glamour and glory but unable to generate any on his own.

The same observer, watching the second six years, would have to change his first take sharply. He would be struck by the resilience and new resolve that animated the young man, by the quickening of his now channeled energies, and by the way he locked into family-created opportunities, using them to enhance both his self-image and his public *persona,* his perceived effectiveness and his own sense of who he had become.

Once through at Harvard, Ted spent the summer of 1956 in the Berber regions of North Africa, with a press card, like his brothers Jack and Bob before him, from the Hearst organization. He traveled with his friend, Harvard instructor Fred Holborn, who acted as his Virgil guiding him through the Dantean circles of colonial Hell and neocolonial Purgatory.

Ted found the beginnings of nationalism in Morocco, Tunisia, and especially Algeria "exciting" and "fascinating." This was his first glimpse of nationalist insurgents and guerillas in action, and his report on it may—as Ted claimed—have influenced his Senator brother to make a dramatic speech urging a French exit from Algeria. More important, it also left an anti-colonial deposit in his own mind that fed his anti-Vietnam feeling and his later dovish foreign policy positions as a Senator.

While Ted was far away with the Berbers and the French Army in Algeria, something important was happening on the Kennedy home front. His brother Jack came a hair's breadth from being chosen as running mate with Adlai Stevenson in his second (1956) campaign against President Dwight Eisenhower. Happily it proved a failure—a kind of "Fortunate Fall," as the early theologians termed it—since the final Stevenson-Kefauver ticket was doomed from the start. Joe Kennedy may have been the Great Father to his sons, but Ike was the Great Father to the whole people.

—— 2 ——

TED returned from his Berber summer to enter the law school of the University of Virginia, at Charlottesville. He had been refused admittance by Harvard Law School, where his brother Joe had gone, doubtless because of his own mediocre and ethically spotted record at Harvard College. The Virginia Law School, which Bob had attended, was more conservative in politics, and no equal of Harvard in its standing, but proud of its traditional honors system. This suggests why—after Ted was initially accepted—there was close to a civil war in the faculty. A general faculty vote finally upheld the dean of admissions' decision, but not without a debate in which family pressures were charged.

Ted did better at law school than at college. He agreed ruefully that he had to study "four times as hard" as the next student. But law studies were concrete and goal-related, while his random scatter of college courses had seemed merely decorative. He "hit the books" as he put it, was lucky in having John V. Tunney, later a Senate colleague from California, to share a house and close friendship with, and—like Bob—was elected head of the law school forum. Granted that his family connections were a factor in the election, since they helped him get forum speakers, it remains true that things were working out for him as never before.

But the earlier, troubled pattern had not wholly been erased. There are no total overnight conversions: Past conduct leaves traces on current conduct. There were at least four instances of encounters with police at Charlottesville because of Ted's reckless driving. One proved serious and strange, since it involved a chase in which Ted outdistanced a police car and, as the police lieutenant later told the story, drove along a side road with lights off, then turned into his driveway where the officer found him "doubled up and hiding in the darkness behind the steering wheel."

We must guard against taking these episodes of Ted's compulsive car speeding too darkly. Clearly they derive from inner needs hidden even from him, and from family and life pressures

on him. There is a willful courting of danger here that Ted displayed also in skiing, mountain-climbing, diving, bobsledding,
flying—at times when he had not prepared himself for his feats.
For Ted it carried with it the romantic self-image of a death-
scorning hero, under some special guardianship of destiny. True,
he lived in a culture that prized daredevil risk-taking; but it also
expected you to take the consequences of your risks.

The Charlottesville occurrence, like the one at Harvard, was
another case of an impulsive, irrational act that triggered consequences beyond its own importance and raised fundamental questions of character. To hide, skulk, and cover up, after the speeding
and the discovery, augured very real character problems. The
episode, minor in itself, very played down by family and prosecutor, is important only because of the shadow it casts ahead to
another and darker event a decade later.

—— 3 ——

DESPITE this, Ted was in a generally upbeat life phase. It was
in this period that he was married to Joan Bennett, whom he met
when he dedicated a Kennedy gymnasium at Manhattanville College, which his sisters attended. It seemed a love match as well as
an appropriate one: Two rich Catholic families were joined, and
Joan was a blonde of picture-book loveliness. Of the three brothers
Bob married first and youngest (at twenty-five), Jack next and
oldest (at thirty-six), Ted closer to Bob (at twenty-seven).

Jack was reluctant to give up the perquisites and delights of
bachelor life until he was already a Senator, looking forward to
the Presidency. Bob's generativity was like the patriarch's: he was
to father eleven children in seventeen years. ("If I had known it
would be a competition," Rose quipped, "I would have kept on
going.") Ted's marriage came just at the time when he had grown
pretty certain of his political vocation. It seemed a romantic case

—as with the English folk song—of one who appeared to know where he was going, and to know also who was going with him. The marriage struck everyone as a felicitous event, with no hint of the troubles ahead.

— 4 —

THE great event after the marriage was Ted's moot court victory. The moot court, in law schools, is a simulated courtroom battle, very like peacetime maneuvers in the Army that put into action the principles taught in the classroom. A Supreme Court Justice, a Federal Appeals judge—and the Lord Chancellor of England too, on a visiting busman's holiday—were the judges for this session, and the trial case dealt with a provision of the Taft-Hartley Act.

Arguing the case, Ted called on his Milton Academy debating skills, marshaling his arguments, presenting them with his impressive presence and vocal resonance. He gave more energy to preparing the moot court case than to his courses, and it was more of a testing of what counted for him, as a trial run in the political vocation he was aiming at. The Kennedy-Tunney team won the competition. Yet whether the judges knew it or not, it was not a lawyer but a politician who was being born.

Ted never became a practicing lawyer. His skills were clearly less legal than political. They radiated from his sheer physical impact, his energy, adaptiveness to people, geniality, and from the consciousness of being a Kennedy.

The vocation of politics was built into each of the brothers and it was what held them together most cohesively in their we-they confrontation with the nameless Adversary in the world outside. The art of politics was something to be mastered by each, with the help of his brothers and father. To fail in this task was to diminish the meaning of the family and deny the sinister reality of the Adversary. The art and vocation of politics took on an almost metaphysical passion.

Thus for Ted to have chosen any vocation other than the political would have been all but unthinkable. It was the family communion, and not to have participated in it would have been to reject equality in the family.

Conversely, to master the skittish, unpredictable wild colt of politics was to *join* the family, no longer as youngest son and brother but as an equal working member. Thus when Jack, planning his second (1958) campaign for the Senate, asked Ted to be his campaign manager, it was like the bestowal of knighthood by the touch of the feudal lord's sword.

— **5** —

TO be sure, it was more nominal than real in any major decision-making sense. As in his first four campaigns, Jack was in summit charge of this one. The operative heads were two of the most skillful of the "Irish Mafia": Ken O'Donnell and Larry O'Brien. The Kennedys had proved themselves masters of the new campaigning. Jack's 1952 Senate campaign was the first truly "scientific" campaign in Massachusetts and one of the first in the United States. It had money, organization, media relations, the mix of amateur volunteers and paid professionals, and an incomparable communication grid. These were the Kennedy signature.

Yet it made sense for Ted to have the post. He was the only available brother—Bobby had to stay with his Washington job—and he could serve as surrogate for Jack at rallies and personal meetings where what was required was the family name and profile. Ted was good at it, and got even more from it than he gave.

But there was also a larger perspective to Ted's campaign job. Surely the patriarch had long thoughts as he watched Ted's growing assurance. He looked ahead to the presidential campaign to which 1958 was a prelude, when (if Jack won) his Senate seat would be vacated and available. Or a governorship might open up. It was unlikely that the Kennedys, who ran scientific campaigns, would fail to do some forward planning for their sequence of political preferment in the family.

At twenty-six Ted might still be the "kid brother" to some, but this was no longer kid stuff. For the Kennedys, despite their quips, politics was the only serious game in town, and it was worth putting the world on notice that a new Kennedy was coming up to join the game. Nor did it hurt when Jack won reelection as Senator by an overwhelming margin.

Every decision in managing Ted's life was now being made with the precision that the Kennedys gave to their campaigns. After his graduation he got the job of running the Rocky Mountain and Western states in Jack's Presidential campaign. His performance in the campaign itself was less than brilliant, with Jack carrying only two of Ted's states and losing California to Nixon.

Yet Ted had found his vocation and won his spurs. The overall margin of victory was perilously narrow, but it was victory, and Ted and Joan took part in the family celebration at the Inaugural. The center of it, as Hero, was the new, crisp, incisive young President. But he must have known that there was another victory, that of the family. Its true hero was the patriarch, whose long dream had come true.

4

Becoming His Own Man: The Path to the Senate

— 1 —

Y ET IT was the eldest son, the President, who sat at the head of the table.

His parents felt fulfilled. "At last," Rose remarked, "the Fitzgeralds have evened the score with the Lodges." And for Joseph Kennedy there was now a new designation in the media: "father of the President." He savored the fruits of what was in essence his victory. He had conceived the idea of it, dragooned the skittish second son into a political career, planned the 1956 vice-presidential effort that made Jack a national figure, and initiated and nourished the running-mate offer to Lyndon Johnson, which was what probably secured the margin of victory.

Here he was now, having heard the new President deliver a strong, stylish Inaugural. Can one doubt, as the Dynast sat there at the Inauguration, that his heart was full? In whatever counted for him his whole nature was to persist and complete. Now he had reached the end he had proposed to himself.

But the Dynast still had two tasks: to make certain that Bob would get his turn at high office—and Ted too. The ambitions for office he had himself abandoned were now worked out in his dynastic impulse. With Jack in the White House, and before anything could happen to the Dynast himself, he had to think of the other two. The ferocious logic of his life, now on its way to fulfillment, was seeking closure.

53

Bob's case wasn't easy. The idea of his taking Jack's Senate seat, or even of running for Governor of Massachusetts, was broached and discarded. It would take time, and Bob was in a hurry. It would mean a move to Boston, and Bob wanted to be in Washington, to make the center hold, lest things fall apart.

Bob was less interested in personal power than in being in the midst of the action. The body must have a center of energy and the center of the political body was in Washington, and its head now was his brother Jack. So the idea of the Attorney-Generalship took shape. At first it was an unthinkable nepotism—or *fraternalism*—and Bob made a show of resisting. "They'll go for our balls if you announce the appointment," he told his brother. "You hold your balls, and I'll announce," the President said.

There was the expected storm, but in time it subsided. The man who was his brother's campaign manager in the election became the watchful guardian of his interests at the critical point where political purpose was translated into the administration of the law—and also, for good measure, where all the federal judges got appointed.

The opposition and also many liberals declaimed against it, but heads of state have often used able brothers at their side. Dynastic politics is older than democracy. All the Kennedy brothers aimed to do was to affect a modern fusion of both.

The President used to quip that he had made his brother Attorney-General so that he could learn some law. The fact was that they both got some education out of it. The Justice post was fated to teach them a good deal they didn't know about civil rights, and to give Bob, and later Teddy, a strong base in black support. The fact was also that Bob turned out to be his brother's best appointment. In addition to running Justice, Bob was (as Arthur Schlesinger put it) the President's "Pooh-Bah, Grand Vizier, and Lord Root of the Matter."

For Edward Kennedy, fresh out of law school, fresh into a marriage and the beginning of a family, freshly plunged into his job as assistant county prosecutor, the axis of his life had shifted sharply. The old bounds that had hedged his life—schools, studies, sports, Army—were broken, and the old sense that he was condemned to live and strive in a lesser world than his brothers was dissipated. One brother was President, the other brother Attorney-General. For the first time he felt close to the kingship principle. Time and fate had moved at a dizzying pace, and the two worlds, his own and his brothers', had become one.

His future became the theme of family discussion. Toward the end of law school his father had told him to go back to Massachusetts and get the political feel of his root community. A job in the Administration was discussed: Joan Kennedy, defending the Senate race later, pointed out that Ted could more easily have taken an Administration job. But his talents were more directly suited to elective politics. The Governorship was considered, and ruled out.

The vacated Kennedy Senate seat was there, physically present, waiting to be claimed. Ted could not be appointed to it by Governor Foster Furcolo: He was too young. There were a number of possible appointees who would have graced the post. But the Kennedys were unlikely to let a Senate seat go to an outsider, however worthy, if it could possibly be kept as a family possession. But who in the family? When the President talked with Governor Furcolo he was careful *not* to say he had Bob in mind, and Furcolo left with the wild conclusion that it was Ted—wild but ineluctable.

The truth is that the President had himself drawn back from his father's proposal to aim at the Senate seat for Ted. It was too naked a power grab to be accepted politically, even with the Kennedy tide running strong. But the father persisted. "You and Bob have both had your turns," he said. "Now it's Ted's turn." Thus was born the "Ted's turn" syndrome that biographers and critics of the Kennedys have fixed on, as expressing the hierarchical thinking of the Kennedys.

The Kennedy commitment to that principle was clear: first and most dramatically in the way a Kennedy would pick up the standard of a fallen brother. But there was another commitment too—that each brother in turn had the right to share in the total political patrimony.

In terms of political theory and theology the two principles were at variance. One followed the doctrine advanced by Robert Filmer and Thomas Hobbes of the primogeniture right of inheritance by the oldest son. The other followed John Locke's theory of the equal division of the inheritance among all the sons. One expressed the monarchical principle, the other the democratic. It was characteristic of the Kennedys that they wanted it both ways, combining both principles in their family polity and in their impact as a dynasty on the popular imagination.

Once the President was convinced, and once the end had been willed, the means were contrived. The Kennedys were not to be stopped by any political niceties. Governor Furcolo was persuaded to appoint Ben Smith, who was Jack's roommate at college, to keep Jack's seat secure until 1962, when Ted would be old enough to run for it.

It was a classic ploy: If Ted were not such a freshly hatched egg the protest would have been manageable. But given his naked lack of experience the sense of outrage, when Ted announced, was as authentic as it was inevitable. The Cambridge liberal establishment, until now loyally in the Kennedy camp, descended on him with all its intellectual artillery, and the political and media leaders across the nation joined them. The Kennedys had expected opposition, but there was an unnerving savagery about this. A justified savagery, since the Kennedy move struck at the prestige of the Upper Chamber and its great traditions.

One must call this testing Ted's first ordeal by fire. In all five phases that followed—the organizing phase before his announcement, the pre-convention phase, the state convention itself, the primary struggle with Edward McCormack, and the election campaign against George Cabot Lodge—he showed a mounting professional competence and a campaigning skill that augured the emergence of a natural political pro.

The campaign and victory were a turning point in his developmental story. It was again his father who had made the campaign possible, and the expectations were that the force and brains behind it would remain Joe Kennedy's. A staff was being put together in the fall of 1961, but before Christmas Joe Kennedy had a stroke, and Ted flew from Boston to Palm Beach to find that a brain clot had paralyzed his father's whole right side and stripped him of the power to walk or talk. What else it did to his powers remained unclear.

Aside from the pain and grief, it did something to Ted Kennedy. It freed him to run his own campaign. There was a fearful pathos in seeing the once laughing, joking, swearing, dominating Dynast sitting there helpless and shriveled in a wheelchair, able to say only "No-no-no-no." Yet the fact was that Ted was now on his own.

True, the campaign organizing had already been planned by the advisers. They had put together, as the Kennedys always did, an effective campaign setup, including the novel addition of a corps of local volunteer "secretaries" for the grassroots work. Ted was briefed and coached on issues by both brothers and by Jack's close aide, Ted Sorensen. But that didn't mean that he was cosseted and swathed in protective wrappings. His organization was the armature, but more and more the decisions were his.

There was an initial skirmish when the Kennedy camp learned that the Boston *Globe* had the Spanish exam-cheating story and was about to break it. From his White House power center Jack maneuvered to kill the story, but failed. There was a compromise and the *Globe* ran an interview in which Ted answered the charge, as he also did in a press release, with carefully worded contrition.

Two of Ted's crucial decisions did require courage. He could have backed away from a floor fight against his Democratic rival, Edward McCormick, at the state convention, but he didn't—and won. When the battle was carried into the primaries he could again have backed away from debating McCormick, especially since the polls showed him well ahead. But he wisely chose not to win too cautiously, but to take some risks and live down the image of a protected rich boy, trading on the reputation and money of his family.

McCormick attacked with verbal brilliance and with the ferocity of a club fighter: He concluded with the famous "If your name were Edward Moore—instead of Edward Moore Kennedy" passage. The effect was curiously one of overkill that turned the sympathy of the voters to Ted as an abused underdog, in place of the intended image of him as a protected rich boy. Containing his anger, as his President brother had strongly advised, and drawing on his considerable debating skills, Ted found that his gamble on the debates paid off. Not that there was anything brilliant or original in his performance: He did a solid job, as he had done in school and college football, in executing the coach's instructions. But the results were satisfying, to the family, himself, and the voters.

His election victory over George Cabot Lodge, his Republican opponent—who said that Ted "ran a perfect campaign"—was by an overwhelming margin. Students of politics puzzled for some years over its meaning, since it broke all the axioms of political science that they had held dear. Ted was too rich, young, inexperienced, and too nakedly the kid brother of the President and Attorney-General. By every tradition of politics—the log cabin, honest work, the principles of merit and experience, the self-made man, the hatred of a privileged elite, the anger at nepotism—the voters should have rejected him soundly.

They didn't. They gave him a rousing endorsement. Why? One explanation was the aristocracy-in-a-democracy theory, which A. A. Michelson, columnist of the Berkshire *Eagle,* expressed as "Everyone loves the Prince"—and the Prince was Ted.

This "Princely Effect" is a halo theory that has Ted profiting by the aura of his brothers. Yet basically it refers to the relationship of sons to a father. In the case of Franklin Roosevelt, who was a king, but none of whose sons reached high office, the standard was never passed. In the case of the Kennedys the father—never himself a king, although a king-maker—identified with his sons, willed their success, and gave them all the power of his psyche, as Roosevelt failed to do. Something in addition was provided by the charismatic Kennedys in their mix of striving, gaiety, risk-taking, and a "Beautiful People" way of life.

But if Ted was representative of the Princely Effect he was also a hard-driving, indefatigable campaigner-Prince whose effort —exactly because he didn't have to make it—was seen as a compliment to the working and middle-class voters. What gift can you give a man who clearly has everything? The answer was: Your vote!

This campaign was, as Murray Levin put it, the first notable experience in contemporary politics with the consequences of voter alienation, which became the most striking feature of the politics of the 1960's and 1970's. It was seen as a recoil from the pieties, pretense, and perfidy of the traditional candidate.

Ted Kennedy was the beneficiary of this strong voter reaction as his brother Jack had been by a less dramatic margin of victory. Voters, it seemed, didn't mind personal or even dynastic politics; they felt disgust with pretense politics. In fact, dynastic politics had one overriding utility: It made it easier to elect constitutional monarchs by the easy transition from aristocracy to majesty.

Without much apparent awareness of it, Ted broke through the bounds of the old politics into a new politics, which became characteristically a Kennedy politics. His brother, the President, who studied Ted's campaign, could only have seen it as a portent of hope for his own reelection. Ted's other brother, Bob, was to add to it in his two campaigns, and make it truly what came to be called the "new politics," with its combination of idealism and hardheadedness, and its appeal at once to the dispossessed, the young, and the blue-collar "ethnics."

It produced a progeny in a whole crop of young candidates in both parties who chose the political vocation, took their cue from the Kennedys, and paid them the ultimate compliment of shaping themselves by their energy, public image, political positions and style.

Chapter III

THE TRIUMPH AND SAVAGING OF THE HOUSE OF KENNEDY

1/The Magus and the Brothers

2/Death of the Brother/Father

3/Ted and Bob: The New Axis, the Final Death

4/The Climate of Tragedy and Legend

1

The Magus and the Brothers

— 1 —

THE STROKE that Joseph Kennedy suffered in December
1961, when Ted's campaign was in its early organizing phase,
freed Ted to take a crucial step in his individuation. But we must
not diminish the scar it left on his mind and memory, nor indeed
the whole complex drama of the relation of father and sons.

It is one of the ancient archetypal dramas of the human
experience. If it is true that family history recapitulates the history
of the race, which in turn is embodied in myth, one would expect
a family history as eventful as the Kennedys' to be illumined by
the great myths.

"This proud, profane, imperious, frank, indiscreet, scheming,
relentless, sensitive, vital man" is how Arthur M. Schlesinger
describes Joseph P. Kennedy. He seems an overpowering father,
but not in the destructive sense, since his identification with his
sons and theirs with him was so strong. Certainly he was a magnetizing and unforgettable father. Like Thomas Jefferson, who
wrote endless letters to his daughter to improve her manners,
deportment, and mind, Kennedy wrote admonishing letters to his
sons, holding them up to the expectations that befitted a family
destined to make history.

If there was an authority problem we have to guess at the
shape it took from fragments available in letters and from remem-

bered conversations with one or another of the brothers. A strong, loving, demanding father interacting with four strong, loving, occasionally rebellious sons: There is bound to be emotional richness there, along with some frictions.

Such an archetypal father in whom the family prehistory was incarnate—identified with his sons, living for and through them —can be described best in terms of the myths he embodied for the sons, consciously or not. He was a Faustian figure, transmitting to them everything in the alembic of the Doctor-Magician: the unquenchable obsession with power and knowledge, the mastery of the environment, the restless movement over the globe, the openess to women's beauty, the drive to sexual domination of them, the courting of danger and death.

But if Joe Kennedy was the Faustus figure, with all its meaning as a prime symbol of the West, he was other Magus figures as well, capable of cunning and craft in the service of his children. He was Prospero, the magician of *A Winter's Tale,* who could summon a castle out of thin air. He was Ulysses, the wanderer, journeying across the continent and seas, always returning laden with tales of the cities and men he had known, bringing back the kindling memories of it to recount to his sons and daughters at the dinner table.

He was also a magician who could do tricks, sometimes stern but also a storyteller with a somewhat heavy humor, and his children became masters of prank and fun and family in-jokes. He could accomplish anything, and around him everything became possible. He encouraged his children, especially his sons, to dream the impossible dream—and to act it out.

There was a more problematic side to this. Having a Magus as father was a temptation to trouble, because along with his other gifts he could always get you miraculously out of trouble by picking up the phone, calling the paper's editor, reaching the police captain or the recruiting colonel, talking always to the man in charge, cajoling, joking, pressuring. He knew everyone, knew where the bodies were buried, was always in on who had done what and who was in whose debt. He was the omniscient and omnipotent father.

The patriarchal family is the model for an effective polity and a strong government. The real thrust of the Kennedys into politics came less from what their father said than from what he was and was not. He was not a moral, values-dominated father. He followed the pragmatic principle that what was good for the family was the right thing to do. Whatever the Kennedys did the rest of their lives, in the high places of politics, they would measure against the father-model engraved deeply in them.

Joe Kennedy tried hard to keep Ted from growing up in an unrealistic elite vacuum. He limited his pocket money, wouldn't give him a bicycle unless his school friends had them too, tried not to let him see himself as a special favored creature. Yet the message somehow came through that he *was* special, that all Kennedys were special.

The father was in truth, like a Daedalus, the "fabulous artificer," for all his sons but for Ted especially, as the youngest and neediest case. For Ted had to be launched with a special urgency, while the paternal power still flowed from the high place, while Jack was still President.

The trouble with such a Daedalus as father was that while sons have to become their father for continuity, they have to be *not their father* if they are to learn what it means to be adult. They are thus caught in a double bind: "Thou shalt be—and thou shalt not be—like thy father."

The Irish family tradition reflects much of this inner debate, because of the heavy Catholic overlay of guilt upon the patriarchal relations. In the Kennedy clan there was never a sharp break or even more than momentary conscious hostility. On the few occasions when we detect echoes of resentment in the Kennedy annals it was always in a framework of love and acceptance. Yet it would be absurd to ignore the inevitable hostility that builds up in the maturing sons of strong fathers.

In his early days Jack had taken his father's lead on policy issues in his honors paper, on the lassitude of the British upper class that left it defenseless against the German technology and war machine. This was compatible, although not identical, with the father's isolationism. "Why England Slept"—which became a moderate success with the promotion help of Joe Kennedy's journalist friend, Arthur Krock—could also fit into an anti-Cliveden conclusion that England could be rescued from its decadent aristocracy only by an aroused people, as happened under Churchill's possessed leadership.

Increasingly Jack's path of thought and his father's diverged. An outward link remained between the son's tough-fibered stand toward Soviet expansion and the father's long-standing anti-Communism, but it was minimal. The son's position was one of engagement, and inherently did't stop short of military showdown, while the father was still confined to his old dream of a fortress America.

The first hairline crack between them showed best in the segment of the young President's Inaugural speech on the challenge of the new generation to the old one. "Let the word go forth from this time and place . . . that the torch has been passed to a new generation of Americans—born in this century, tempered by war, disciplined by a hard and bitter peace, proud of our ancient heritage." There was no burden this America wouldn't bear, he told the world, no sacrifice it wouldn't risk to maintain freedom, and he challenged the young generation to "ask not what your country can do for you—ask what you can do for your country."

It was, from the standpoint of his own "mid-life individuation," as Jung called it, the most significant passage in the Inaugural. We must read it not only as a President's message to the nation and world but as a son's message to his father's generation—and doubtless to his father himself. We must also envisage the impact of this challenge on his youngest brother and *his* generation. Ted, not yet twenty-nine, just out of law school, was stirred by the miraculous fact of Jack's being President, and eager to join him in the young men's task of governing.

At some point early in his Administration the President spelled out his generational Declaration of Independence more explicitly to his father, who still pressed him on one issue or another. He made it unmistakably clear that his views were his own, in words that must have burned themselves into the mind of the old man, whose pride in his son was matched by a touchy pride of his own. John Kennedy didn't like to push anyone, but he didn't like to be pushed either, even by his father.

It was a poignant expression of the painful passing of power as generation succeeded generation. It was also an historical turning point in the whole family polity of the Kennedys. It legitimized Bob's earlier rebellion when, against his father's advice, he abandoned his job with the McCarthy Committee and later joined his brother in the more congenial task of exposing the labor corruption of Dave Beck and Jimmy Hoffa.

It was even more a turning point for Ted, who had never himself broken with his father's political thinking but followed his brothers' lead in his campaigning for Jack in 1958 and 1960.

Clearly there was a new family head. "The King is dead. Long live the King." The father was still father but with Jack as "Mr. President" the locus of family authority shifted. Ted's love for his father was unchanged, but his dazzled admiration was for his brother, and his primary identification figure shifted.

The shift had in one sense started earlier. In Jack's first congressional campaign the father was a felt and observed presence, holding the purse strings pretty visibly, bringing his old associates into command positions, changing strategies and making tactical decisions. With each successive campaign his Old Guard found itself replaced by the New Guard forming itself around Jack and Bob—a mixture not quite as before, of hard-driving amateur-pros, culminating in Bob's management of the presidential campaign.

During one of Ted's chores in that campaign he did a reckless ski-jump. He explained to friends later that he had really wanted to "take off my skis and go down the side." But if Jack had heard of it, "I know I would be back in Washington, licking stamps and envelopes." The surrogate-father was in firm command, at least in Ted's mind.

For sufficient reasons Jack had to keep his father under wraps —to mute the talk of bought elections, to keep him out of the hair of the younger men, to protect himself from the continuing memory of the ambassador's isolationist years and his too close cozying with appeasement groups both in England and the United States.

Joe Kennedy reasserted his authority twice: once when he carried the day on Lyndon Johnson as Jack's running mate, against Bob's bitter opposition, and again when he convinced his President son to go along with Ted's Senate candidacy. But in both instances the aging Court counselor was clearly appealing to the new young King, and was not the King himself.

Launching Ted's campaign was his last clear-minded political act. It was going well, and he had largely retired from the campaign. We know pathetically little about what triggered the blood clot in his brain. He had more mental peace than he ever had, with his two sons in power and the third on his way, with all three close and working together. What other man of his age had as much right to feel that his life dream had been fulfilled?

The stroke came thus at the high moment of his life. As befitted a man who had always felt himself in control, he refused to have a doctor called. He was overruled. Ted flew down to Palm Beach from Boston with a specialist, and Jack and Bob flew from Washington. Things would never be the same for anyone.

The old man was to stay in his wheelchair for almost eight years. The primal father, stricken, was no longer the Magus. His boys were still his sons, and they watched over him with love, retained him in his place at the table at most family gatherings, tried to guess from his repeated "No-no-no-no-no's" what was going on in his mind. But they were on their own now, less sons than a band of brothers.

2

Death of the Brother/Father

— 1 —

IN THEIR role playing some men are primarily sons and remain sons most of their lives, others become fathers, with a feel for power and for their children. Still others focus on peer relationships and remain brothers.

In Ted's case the passage from being a son to being a brother established his dominant life mode. The shift of family authority that had begun with Jack's election to the Presidency was completed by the father's stroke. Along with their grief over the sadness of it, the three brothers could also make a final breakaway from the father's authority.

It may have been hardest for Jack, who found himself thrust into the double role of being the new head of the clan as well as of the nation. He was beset from without by Nikita Khrushchev, who crowded and tried to cow him, and by Fidel Castro, who competed with him for the commitment of the young in the West. His image, in his mid-forties, was publicly that of the radiant and maturing world leader. But his image in terms of his private life —aside from his marriage and children—was that of the erotically focused male enjoying the risks of sexual adventure along with the power game of world politics. Being out in front, he had to take final responsibility for decisions of state. Having one brother as working partner and another as brother/son must have placed an added emotional burden on him.

Along with his father, Ted always had the eldest brother—first Joe Jr., then Jack—as the next in the hierarchy of authority, the one who transmitted the parental standards. In that sense Ted always had two fathers, two authority figures, as Bob had also. Now Ted had a single functioning authority, one so busy being national leader that Ted was thrown increasingly on his own.

He thrived on it. The two years between his father's stroke and Jack's death were productive years for him, perhaps the freest and least anxious of his life. At the start of 1963 he dug into his Senate work, learned the rules, used his considerable adaptive skills to win the confidence of Senate leaders, including the Southern conservatives who dominated the Senate "club" and who at first resented his youth, his inexperience, and his being a Kennedy. No one coming to the Senate, fresh and young, had ever been more "correct" in gauging what was expected of him and what limits he had to set for himself. He made no speeches, touched all bases, and learned where the Senate's power centers were located.

This was also the initial year when, as leader of the Democratic party in Massachusetts, he set about reorganizing and tidying up the State party structure, striking a power balance between the on-the-spot professionals and an advisory group of academic liberals. It was the initial year when he began shaping what was to become one of the ablest, best functioning of Senate staffs.

He seemed set for a long Senate career, with whatever else was to accompany it as his brother Jack moved through his first term and doubtless a second, and—who could tell?—as his brother Bob possibly succeeded him in 1968. Did he dream of following Bob? The not impossible succession of the three brothers in the White House was in everyone's mind, cropping up in the columns, a constant item in the joking cocktail and barroom talk; it would be surprising if Ted didn't sometimes savor the thought during the three vibrant, event-packed years from November 1960 to November 1963. By 1976 he would still be only forty-four, in young maturity. If he were as literary as his brothers he might have thought of Wordsworth's lines: "Joy was it in that dawn to be alive/And to be young was very Heaven."

— 2 —

THE dawn turned to darkness precipitously with the almost mythical death of the hero. The story has often been told of how the news of President Kennedy's assassination in Dallas reached his young brother in the Senate chamber. Ted was in the chair, presiding, a chore often assigned to freshmen Senators. He was using the time to sign a mass of correspondence, scarcely listening to the droning voice of the Senator of the moment. A press-liaison officer rushed through the chamber, reached the dais with the news. "Your brother the President. He's been shot!"

"No!" The immediate denial and warding off. Then the impulse to action. To get the latest wire news of Jack's condition, to get to Bobby. But neither was easy, or even possible, in that panicky, rumor-filled capitol. It was a nightmare of frustration. Here was a U.S. Senator, brother of the President who had just been shot, yet he couldn't find a functioning telephone anywhere, not even at his home: the phones were dead or the extensions he wanted were busy. He finally reached Bob at Hickory Hill, who confirmed the death. Bob's assignment to Ted was to see to the family at Hyannisport. Ted reached his mother, who was fearful about how his father would take the news. He flew to Hyannisport, and confronted the task of how to break it to him.

For Joseph Kennedy, who had sat staring blankly into vacant space after Joe Jr.,'s death and Kathleen's, there was never the final acceptance of death as passage that devoted Catholics have, and which Rose was able to achieve. But if the father never accepted the deaths he may have managed some partial solace by throwing all his energies into Jack's career. It would be the vindication of his shattered hope. How do you now tell this already stricken father that the vindicating son has himself been killed?

It became a grim game that the family played with the old man the rest of the day and evening, and Ted—never one for sharp decisions and quick confrontations—joined in the game, delaying the final word. The father, his sharpness not wholly dimmed by the stroke, sensed that something was being kept from him. He had to be calmed and his efforts at discovery circumvented: At one point Ted ripped the connecting wires from the TV set to put it out of action. The next day Ted told him. The father took it hard, but he took it. He wanted to go to Washington for the funeral, but finally settled for watching it on TV.

Everyone else in the nation watched the hero being borne to his rest. The funeral was deeply affecting, at once a solemn pageant and a collective purging. It expressed the country's loss and the family's grief. As the American people watched it on TV it offered the stylized solemnity which could in some measure channel the shock and pain.

But it was too massive a pageant, and the death itself too staggering and absurd to be grasped by those close to the slain man. Ted was not one for open demonstrations of grief. There were a few wry touches—an exchange in the limousine between Jacqueline Kennedy and Bob about whether John, Jack's little son, should wear gloves ("Boys don't wear gloves," said Bob); the canvassing of close friends about whether the coffin should be open or closed (they voted to have it closed); the rented dress suit for Ted arriving without pants or hat, a mishap mended by letting out the President's pants; and, Ted's head size being too big for a quick substitution, his decision to walk hatless, which was forthwith matched by a hatless procession of captains and kings, from DeGaulle down.

These were the curiously displaced bits and pieces, later noted and remembered, serving (in Eliot's phrase) as the "objective correlates" of the emotion that would ring false if expressed more directly. The Kennedys didn't like emotional directness: Their style was marginal, glancing, averted. Ted shared in it. He found in *Ecclesiastes* an opening text for the officiating bishop:

"To everything there is a season . . . A time to be born, a time to die." But unlike Bob's quotable lines during those harsh and hopeless days, there are few attributed to Ted.

—— 3 ——

HE doubtless felt the sharp sense of loss, of what might have been, as much as the rest did. But where Bob turned to the Greek tragic texts, to find sources of solace and renewal, that was not Ted's way. He plunged back into the details, the wonderfully distracting details, of his work as Senator. That, he felt, was how Jack would have wanted it.

He had much to block out of his mind. "Anyway, three years is better than nothing," Bobby said after the killing. Those three years had been good for Ted, yes, but not what they had been for Bob, because the two younger brothers had different relationships with the President. Bob lost a brother and an intimate working partner—almost a *camarado* in Walt Whitman's joyous sense of the word. Ted lost a more distant brother/father. There was a fifteen-year difference between them—a generation, as generations are measured in the frames of intellectual and values climates. Bob came just halfway between them, bridging them.

This sheds light on the differing reactions of the two brothers to the President's death. As Arthur Schlesinger, Jr. tells of Bob's response—at first shocked, then sardonically bitter, then one of intense self-exploration and wide reading—the overall effect is one of testing and even transformation. One sees a man, not quite turned forty, stricken ("Why, God?"), fumbling for answers to an unanswerable riddle, but in the process reaching an adult sense of his own strength as well as his vulnerability.

It is hard to find evidence of anything comparable in Ted. At the start of his thirties, just getting into his work, with shaky and erratic years behind him, Ted needed the supportive interest and oversight of both his brothers to move toward adulthood. Now the brother/father, the symbolic base on whom he had counted for help, had been cut away, and everything crumpled.

Had it happened ten years later, when he had more life experience and grown surer of himself, he might, like Bob, have responded with greater inner growth. As it was, the effective loss of his father and the death of his surrogate father, so close together, took a heavier toll on his inner resources than anyone could foretell.

3

Ted and Bob: The New Axis, the Final Death

— 1 —

A STORY ABOUT Bob and Ted, by Peter Maas: Bob went to a Christmas party for an orphanage a few weeks after Dallas. A little black boy, of six or seven, stepped up to him and said, "Your brother's dead, your brother's dead." There was a shocked silence, and the little boy, feeling he had said something wrong, began to cry. Bob "picked him up. . . . held him very close . . . and he said, 'That's all right, I have another brother.' "

It is a story worth retelling because it captures both the heartbreak of Jack's death and the relationship left for the two remaining brothers to develop.

So much depended on it, for both men. They needed each other. Yet for Bob especially it couldn't be the same. The sense of joyous, rollicking collusion, in an almost unparalleled brother-brother power relationship, playing for the highest stakes against an Adversary world: That was gone, and could never be recaptured. Bob could never find another Jack, nor could he be Jack, even if he became President.

Inevitably Jack's death intensified Bob's interest in the Presidency. It was, after all, the family Grail. The night of the Inauguration, Jack had given Bob a cigarette case with the inscription, "After I'm through, how about you?" Now Bob moved to vindicate and complete Jack's work.

75

For Ted this had its own peculiar difficulty, because he couldn't play Bob to Bob's Jack, and because the thrust toward the Grail wasn't in him. He was a spirited, concrete-minded fellow, limited in ways that his brothers were not, and at times almost pedestrian. What he needed from Bob was another father/brother axis, but closer than the one Jack had given him.

For almost five years they worked at it, Bob pursuing his own self-examining struggle for a clear political direction, counting on Ted to furnish the earthy foundation on which together they could rebuild the cloud-capped Kennedy castle.

As Attorney-General, Bob went through an embittered tactical struggle with Lyndon Johnson in which the young Senator from Massachusetts couldn't help him much, despite the fact that Johnson liked Ted best—or disliked him least—of the three brothers. But Bob's hard decisions on civil rights in running the Justice Department did serve as spinoff learning experiences for Ted.

After a harrowing time of intrigue and maneuver in both camps—his own and LBJ's—Bob finally abandoned his hopeless quest for the vice-presidential spot on Johnson's 1964 ticket. Thus one path toward regaining the Presidency for the Kennedys was closed off. Bob then took the only reasonably quick path open, making his "carpetbagger" campaign for a Senate seat from New York against the liberal Republican incumbent, Kenneth Keating. It took a hard-driving single-purposed resolve to win the seat, awakening as it did a double set of memories: of Ted's "starting at the top" in his Massachusetts bid for the Senate, and of Bob's "ruthlessness" as Attorney-General and earlier as counsel for the labor rackets investigation. It confirmed many in their conviction that a Kennedy would stop at little to get his way.

My own memories of the Senate campaigns of both brothers may suggest the mood of the time. Along with others I had attacked the family decision to run Ted for the Senate in 1962 as an instance of high arrogance, given Ted's rawness of knowledge or experience. By 1964 I supported Bob for the Senate, despite his quick shift of residence. As a national figure he had lived as much in New York as in Washington and Virginia. His four years as close co-worker with the slain President, I thought, gave him a high platform from which to make his try at the Presidency. I cite these memories because they reflect how different the storms were that raged around the two Kennedy senatorial campaigns, in 1962 and 1964.

As it turned out, both men were elected to their Senate seats in 1964—Ted for a full term, Bob for the first time—and Ted by a much bigger margin than Bob.

— 2 —

BOB was living on two levels, the political and philosophical. On one he was entangled in the narrow and nasty infighting with his brother's successor, Lyndon Johnson, in which both men, with a deep hatred of each other, displayed the spitefulness of little boys on the public stage.

On the second level he was sorting out what meaning Jack's death could have for his own life. After a spell of depression his essentially affirmative spirit asserted itself in two ways. He came to insist on a highly idealized version of what his brother's tenure of power had stood for, in terms of caring primarily about the insulted and the injured. He decided also to aim at the high office where power, used with skill and concern, could undo the inequities and inequalities of the defenseless, and thus give meaning both to Jack's death and to his own life as survivor.

Ted in time adopted the direction Bob took, in tandem with him. But Ted had little of the intuitive and even mystical that were combined, in a strange mixture with a feral scrappiness, in Bob. With Bob slightly in the lead the two Senators reached in time the same basic positions on civil rights, civil liberties, welfare state programs, and foreign policy. But the bitterness and, for a time, alienation that Bob worked out philosophically, Ted had to cope with existentially, in action.

He didn't talk as wildly as Bob did, during the first weeks and months after the assassination, but he lived wildly. He didn't say "Why, God?", and question the very basis of existence, but he acted out his sense that not much of what happened had much meaning. There was an implied defiance in his drinking and driving. There was more gossip than before about his extramarital sexual wanderings. For him there was no functioning father left, either in the Kennedy family or in the universe.

You did your work well, tended to your political fences, ran a good staff in Washington and a good Massachusetts operation: That was tangible and concrete, the job of a pro. You followed Bob's lead on issues and stands: He had the brains and experience. But beyond that you moved fast, seized your pleasures where you could, and guarded yourself against strong emotions and deep commitments, because the people you had loved got killed or taken away, and there was no point to asking for more pain. So Ted—a kind of *homme moyen sensuelle*—dug into action, speed, pleasure, and concrete accomplishment.

—— 3 ——

EARLY in June 1964 he stayed late for important Senate business, and then had to get to Springfield where the Massachusetts Democratic Convention was waiting to nominate him again by acclamation. He was tired, anxious, under pressure. His friends, Senator and Mrs. Birch Bayh, and his close aide Ed Moss, were with him on his private plane. The weather was closing in, the ceiling was low, but Ted was determined to get to the convention, and against advice he told the pilot to take off. The plane crashed, Moss and the pilot were killed, and Ted so badly hurt that there was question about whether he would be paralyzed permanently. The Bayhs escaped with minor injuries. Ted was in the hospital for months, including the time of the campaign and election, and still bears his back injury.

It could have happened to anyone. It did happen to Ted Kennedy, less than seven months after his brother's death. There was dark talk in the media about the "curse" that pursued the Kennedys.

Ted had plenty of time to ponder the curse and other questions as he lay mending in the New England Baptist Hospital. The Massachusetts voters gave him the most massive margin of victory in the state's history—almost 75 percent of the vote. Bob, who had come to visit him in the hospital ("Is it true you're ruthless?" the battered Ted asked him) had squeezed through in the New York election, ironically saved by LBJ's "coattails" while Ted ran well ahead of Johnson. How much of Ted's higher margin of victory was for his two years of Senate performance, how much for sympathy on his crash, how much for his running—unlike Bob—in his home state, we cannot know.

But another chapter had been written in the script of the family destiny and legend. With the two early deaths, the father's stroke, Jack's killing, Ted's crash, the legend of some unique and fatal personal doom became fixed in the popular mind. At the same time, with both the surviving brothers now in the Senate, the other side of the legend—that of some unique political destiny— was also emerging.

— 4 —

THE two brothers took their oath of office as Senator together in 1965. In legislative experience Ted was two years the senior, in administrative experience and intellectual dazzle Bob was way ahead. Yet by the consensus of historians Ted was the better Senator. Bob's was a perfunctory performance. His heart simply wasn't in it. He used the Senate largely as a staging ground for the Presidency, and he was in a hurry.

It was an ideal brother axis. Ted focused largely on domestic policy, giving his maiden Senate speech on the poll tax some eighteen months after his first election, and following it with carefully prepared, courageous measures on civil rights, school desegregation, one-man-one-vote reapportionment. There was a fraternal division of labor. Bob concentrated largely on foreign policy, growing ever more dovish on the Vietnam War, breaking away from President Johnson when it became evident that Johnson was locked into a rigid position on the war, and that anyone displacing him in 1968 would have to do it on the war issue.

On any overview it was clear that Bob was moving rapidly toward the Left of the liberal spectrum, and that Ted—more slowly, especially on the war—was moving after him.

Along with his President brother, Bob had been surprised by the intensity of feeling among the black intellectual and political leaders whom they had brought to the White House for discussion. Ever sensitive to nuances of change, Bob saw that the President and he would have to cope with civil rights in a major way. It was part of John Kennedy's growth to political maturity that he came to understand the pace and intensity of the civil rights movement instead of setting himself stonily against it. Lyndon Johnson, in his own way and with Bob's help, carried this farther into the Civil Rights Voting Act, and Ted now took it over as one of his central legislative tasks.

It was a turning point in the history of the American liberal consciousness, and Ted was an important part of it, if not an initiating force.

While he was in enforced captivity at the New England Baptist Hospital after his accident, he had a stream of visitors from the liberal faculty of Harvard and MIT, visitors like Ken Galbraith, Sam Beer, and Jerome Wiesner, and was given a highly condensed post-graduate course in economics, history, foreign policy, nuclear science, and weapons systems. Only his plight, and who he was, could have focused such a large-scale educational effort on one young Senator. He was exposed to the best conventional wisdom of the Eastern Intellectual Establishment.

Ted was more at home with the Kennedy politics than with the Kennedy world view, which shifted considerably over the years. He was too young to have been exposed to the family's prewar isolationism in the late 1930's, and he was on the margin of Jack's and Bobby's war and postwar thinking in the 1940's. His own schooling came in the Cold War climate of the 1950's, and his Senatorship in the planetary turmoil of the early 1960's, experienced by Jack and Bob at the White House summit and by Ted at secondhand through them.

Deeply involved in political warfare and "counterinsurgency" efforts, Bob came to be known as even more of a "cold warrior" than his brother the President—a designation he would have to live down. His experience in foreign policy decision-making was during the Cuban missile crisis of 1962, when he headed Excom, the President's special task force that sat continuously during the tense two weeks of the crisis. It was a hairy period of high risk and stakes for both the President and his brother, a maturing time for both.

Ted had not been greatly involved in these actions and passions before Jack's death, and even after it he tended to stick to domestic issues. But as Bob moved into an anti-war position, from 1965 to 1967, Ted did too, although on a lower key.

—— 5 ——

WHAT interested him more was the political dilemma Bob was caught in: whether to run or not to run against Lyndon Johnson in 1968. This dimension of tactical judgment was very much Ted's province, and he joined Bob in exploring it. Part of its importance for Ted's future lay in its being the experimental proving ground for his own later efforts—from 1968 to 1980—to canvas opinion, reach a decision, and lay plans for his own presidential candidacy.

Bob, passionate and decisive in taking stands on civil rights and the Vietnam War, was curiously hesitant about making the run to knock Johnson out of office. He was convinced that the war was morally wrong as well as politically impossible. Yet he could not bring himself to an open break with the Johnson loyalists, who included some of his best friends. He told those who pressured him to run—among them notably Allard Lowenstein, in September 1967—that he could not be responsible for dividing the Democratic party, and would probably get beaten in the process. Besides, he was confident that if he wanted it he could get the nomination less expensively in 1972. Whatever his boldness in policy, he was prudent in political decisions.

Ted, who had been given the job of canvassing Bob's friends and supporters on the run-or-not issue, ended by supporting Bob's judgment. Both men felt that the "realistic" thing to do was wait. Ted later made a revealing comment about his father and dead brother on this score: "Dad would have said, 'Don't do it.' Jack would have cautioned . . . against it, but he might have done it himself."

But it was a case of miscalculating the larger and deeper reality—the mood of the people and their readiness for change. Both brothers missed out on understanding the unparalleled currents of social upheaval in the society.

The sixties were a scarred and scarring decade in American life, probably the most revolutionary in the nation's history, in its headlong pace of change, the accelerations in every phase of life, the cold and hot wars, the activist and protest movements, the breakthrough in values systems and in cultural styles. The spirit of the time furnished both the frame and outcome of what happened to the Kennedys. They were the product of the decade, and part of its dynamic, but they had to understand that dynamic.

Politics were no longer the monopoly of the professionals, including the liberal Kennedy types. At Columbia, C. Wright Mills was exploring the emergence of a new and young intellectual class, blacks and whites, mostly students, who were moving to take over the levers of power. His *Letter to the New Left* was addressed to a new radical liberal—young, energetic, passionately committed—whose springs of action and belief were anti-Establishment. In a youth-oriented, media-ridden multileveled society, there was an accelerative principle at work in the minds of those who counted. Each change in the perception of reality fed on the expectation of deeper and sharper changes to come.

This was happening also in the dynamics of the war and in anti-war feeling. Senator Eugene McCarthy—cooler, subtler, more intellectual and also more cynical than Bob Kennedy—took up Lowenstein's challenge, entered the New Hampshire primary, recruited whole armies of the invading young, and got enough of the vote to thrust Johnson out of the race. Both the Kennedys discovered ruefully that their prudence and "realism" had misled them. They had read the signs wrong.

— 6 —

AWAKENED from his dreamy dance of indecision Bob Kennedy now moved fast into the presidential campaign, like a suitor who sees his beloved about to take the vow with a rival and bursts into the church to claim the bride for himself. He admitted that McCarthy's surprise showing in New Hampshire had propelled him into the race, but he argued that he could win and McCarthy couldn't.

The "New Class" of students, militants, intellectuals, artists, and the young were generally sharply split by the struggle between the two anti-war candidates. Bob was at a disadvantage in wooing the newly emerged group of committed activists because he had come in late, and seemed to validate the charges of Kennedy arrogance and his own ruthlessness. For the first time the Kennedy control over the allegiance of the liberal political avant-garde was in doubt.

Bob put Ted loosely in charge of his campaign. But actually there was no single sovereign director with a clear-cut chain of command, but rather a cluster of shifting suzerainties, under Ken O'Donnell, Ted Sorensen, Steve Smith, and Lawrence O'Brien, presided over by Ted. For both brothers the 1968 campaign was a nightmare of improvisations, snares, obstacles, missed chances, makeshift and chaotic organization. The precision and easy mastery of change and circumstance that everyone had come to expect from a Kennedy campaign were simply not there.

The fierce control that Bob had himself exercised over Jack's 1960 presidential campaign was not there either, now that Bob was himself the candidate. Nor was Ted's previous experience as titular head of Jack's 1958 Senate campaign much of a preparation. Everything had been planned for him in 1958, and the Kennedys had then been moving on an ascending arc of confidence and acceptance. While Ted handled the campaign well in some states like Indiana, he had on the whole neither the personal authority to impose himself as campaign manager, nor could he evoke the national acceptance essential for an effective campaign.

The fact was that after Jack's death, less than five years earlier, the Kennedy magic could no longer be taken for granted. The New Left questioned the Kennedy radical credentials; the peace groups found Gene McCarthy purer than Bob; the academics liked McCarthy's intellectual style; the unions, mistrustful of Bob, recalling his prosecutorial role in the labor rackets investigation, supported Hubert Humphrey who was quietly gathering delegate strength as a moderate alternative to both Bob and McCarthy.

The Kennedys had known they would be in for a struggle but had not calculated it would be this hard. Ted, on better terms with McCarthy than Bob, tried to negotiate a peace settlement with him but to no avail. Bob was a rough club-fighter, but McCarthy had the student cohorts and exasperated the Kennedys with a deflationist wit that they had considered a family monopoly.

Bob did best in the Indiana primary, finding exactly the New Politics mix that appealed both to inner city blacks and hardbitten white ethnics. He had other victories as well, but Pennsylvania's city bosses and union leaders turned a stony face to the Kennedys. Oregon—upper-middle class, suburban, with a high educational level—was clearly McCarthy territory, and the Kennedy forces compounded their disadvantage by an unbelievable organizational muddle. A good deal rode on Oregon, and the results were a wounding defeat.

It was seen as a serious Kennedy campaign defeat. The spell of the Kennedy legend was cracking. The mystique of efficiency, effortless victory and a special grace no longer operated. But Bob counted on a California victory to keep him "viable" (a hapless term, blurted out in the verbal squalor of battle) until the convention itself, when the Kennedys hoped to use their vaunted floor skills to restore the lost élan. California was better territory for Bob than Oregon because it was pluralist, polyglot, as various as America itself.

Ted was on the California battle scene where Bob campaigned at fever pitch, using every weapon of rhetoric, tactic, and appeal at his command. Bob's mood was tense and electric, and as the days passed his buoyancy returned and with it his special charisma. Defeat was unthinkable. In the end he squeezed out a victory over McCarthy, not by a glorious margin but a victory nonetheless.

— 7 —

HE was taking a shortcut through a hotel kitchen in Los Angeles on his way to a celebration after a victory announcement when Sirhan Sirhan's gun put an end to the campaign. It stilled the ever active mind and cut short his seemingly invincible life force.

It put an end also to the closest, deepest relationship that Ted Kennedy had ever had, when for almost five years the two younger Kennedy brothers planned and acted together, stood together in sorrow, victory, and in gathering adversity, and formed a truer partnership than Ted was ever again to know.

4

The Climate of Tragedy and Legend

— 1 —

THE KENNEDYS have always taken their deaths gallantly and they had deaths enough to take. They had come to expect that life would break their hearts, and each time they rallied for the next round, whether of life or death.

Ted had just addressed a San Francisco victory celebration, and he and his close aide, Dave Burke, were in their hotel suite and had turned on the TV to watch Bobby's announcement. What they saw sent them scurrying on an Air Force plane to Los Angeles where Ted kept watch for a day over his dying brother at the Good Samaritan Hospital. Then he flew the coffin back to Washington, to the sad and now too familiar rituals of death and national bereavement.

He refused to let go emotionally. He was head of the family now and had to stay in charge. There was one thing he kept saying to the newsmen on the plane with him: "I'm going to show them what they've done, what Bobby meant to this country, what they lost." It was the Kennedy response to a loss, what Bob did when Jack died, what the father had done when Joe Jr. died: use it as a spur to fill the loss and vindicate the life and promise of the dead.

Ted never explained who he meant by "they" and "them." He didn't have to. It was true that Sirhan Sirhan killed Robert Kennedy amidst the hotel steam tables. But it is just as true that "they" played a part in the killing. The electric two-way attraction between the Kennedys and "them" has been one of the mysteries of American political history. Each was magnet to the other, fed the other.

Bob had experienced the deaths of two of his brothers—one by public murder—yet he had again pursued the phantom public until it turned to destroy him. Ted experienced the public murder of the last two of his brothers, yet his vow after the second killing was to "show them"—which he could do only by pursuing and wooing them.

Ted felt wounded, and inevitably felt the guilt of the survivor. He is gone, I am here. Why he, not I? As Bob's closest adviser and campaign manager, he had to ask himself what he and Bob could have done differently, what choices they could have made that would not have ended up in the blood and wrack of the hotel passageway?

The decade of the sixties was the fateful one for the three Kennedy brothers. Jack was elected President at its start and was killed when it was a third over. Bob was elected Senator and began serving halfway through, and was dead four-fifths of the way through. Ted was elected and reelected and almost killed in his crash in the first half, and got involved in his historic Chappaquiddick "incident" before the last year was over.

The time after Bob's death was one of great confusion for Ted, as he was torn in several directions. There were his responsibilities as the new head of the family, now augmented by Bob and Ethel's children, and his obligations to his stricken father. There was his Senate career, which now seemed a haven from the storms, a place where his special talents could be effective. There was the pull of his private life, at times now a pretty public one, which he may have sought as a relief from tension and was reluctant to give up. But, overriding them all, there was also his sense of duty, to his father and the memory of his brothers, which would inevitably lead to risk and grief if he should in his turn ever try for the Presidency.

His father wept pitifully at the death of the third son for

whom he had dreamt once more the dream of ultimate power and honor. How could Ted, himself torn by grief, guilt, and doubt, solace him?

— 2 —

OF all the patriarch's mythic forms that of Daedalus proved the most fitting. The "fabulous artificer" had contrived wings for each Icarus son—for Joe Jr., for Jack, for Bob—to fly superbly into glory, and the hot sun of war and violence had melted the wings and sent each to his death on the rocks below. It was a case of paying with death for the hubris of what he had dared attempt.

Now the father sat nursing his grief over Bob, pondering the fate of his family. Here was his last son sitting with him, a massive presence, radiating energy, the only remaining carrier of the family vocation. Could he break the tragic pattern, carry the family at last to the place for which it had paid so dearly, complete what his brothers had begun? The repeated "no-no-no" that emerged from the torrent of words the old man tried to utter was delphic in its meaning. But Freud had once said that "the little word No" is the hallmark of Death.

Ted was not given to introspection. But as he sat with his father and looked back over his life, he could remember no time, until now, when he had not been buffered by the protection of his father and brothers. He had had four fathers, the natural father paired with the eldest son as surrogate in succession. For the youngest child there was some comfort, because with each death he could turn to another father for support, lessening the trauma. And even when the patriarch himself was stricken he first had Jack as a father/brother, and after him Bob. Now he had no one, except an inconsolable old man.

For Ted, as for many boys in growing up, the father was also a hero figure. Each brother in succession became also the family hero figure and therefore his. To have too many fathers makes it harder to become an adult. To have too many heroes makes it both more necessary and more difficult to make the transition to oneself as hero.

— 3 —

THERE had been a dream-laden quality about Ted's apprentice years, along with the problematic and tragic. Ted could look back at the bittersweet pageant of his life with some relish, especially the years since he had been able to join with Jack and Bob in their campaigns. They had been a vibrant, tough company of brothers, with their jesting and jousting, their hard sports and hard jokes, their hurts and horseplay, their competitiveness that sometimes turned hostile, their shared triumphs and defeats, and above all their common front against an intrusive world.

They were—in the term Geza Roheim used about kinship relations in the Australian tribes—the "eternal ones of the dream." They knew their own and each other's roles so well that it could be said they dreamt each other's dream. On one level it was a communal dream of authority and rebellion, on another a dream of obstacles and resistance, of death and fears of death, and of flight and recovery in the face of fear.

They were all primarily actors rather than thinkers, particularly Ted. Their concern was with the political theater around them. They lived intense personal lives but for them the realm of public service was the stage that counted, and they didn't feel truly alive unless they were on stage. They were constantly before the camera. Ted was before the camera from the time he was an ambassador's son. They came to power during the emergence of TV as the great political medium, and they were superbly fitted to use it and be used by it.

—— 4 ——

TED didn't write the eulogy he delivered for his brother Bob at
St. Patrick's Cathedral, nor did he give his writers any directions
except to say he wanted "something about love." He was not a
man of words. But while his best speechwriter, Milton Gwirtzman, was probably responsible for the extraordinary cadences, the
vision of Bob in the speech was one that Ted felt deeply—that he
was "a good and decent man who saw wrong and tried to right
it, saw suffering and tried to heal it, saw war and tried to stop it."

While it was all true about the Bob whom Ted had idealized,
it wasn't the entire truth. Bob was also a polarizer in a polarizing
time. It must be said of him—what cannot be said of Jack—that
he helped create the climate of tension that pervaded the era of
his death. More than any of his brothers Bob was Adversary-
oriented. He had more of a feel for the symbolic than Ted did and
was more of an absolutist than Jack, looking always for a cause
and fighting its opponents as his enemies.

This sense of politics as the art of finding and fighting the
enemy had never wholly left him, which may be why he felt at
home in his early investigative work, and later in fighting civil
rights cases as Attorney-General, and still later in his senatorial
and campaign battles. He shifted his causes but remained enemy-
oriented. There was something of the Savonarola in Bob, especially in the heat of a campaign—a certitude that God would
trample his and the nation's enemies because he was on God's
side.

There was a rage sweeping through the land during the five
years that included Jack's death and Martin Luther King's and
finally Bob's. The last two—King's and Bob's—came close together. Both were a reflection of the anger of the time. The burning
cities became the funeral pyres of both men, both victims of the
climate of violence and tragedy.

Each man was a leader during his life and became a legend
with his death. In the case of both Kennedys, as in King's case,

the legend was fed not only by martyrdom but by the widespread sense that the truth about the deaths had not been told—that it had been covered up by nefarious men, that just as there had been a conspiracy to kill, so there had been a conspiracy to conceal.

Ted knew that Bob had never believed in the conspiracy theory about Jack's death. The death itself was so shattering that anything that attempted to explain it seemed puny and extraneous. Ted felt much the same about Bob's death, and refused to get involved with the many ingenious theories that spun themselves around it. Each of the brothers had been a lusty fighter, none was paranoid.

Yet the conspiracy theories about each of the Kennedy murders deepened the mystique attaching to the family. The whole swirling controversy about "Who killed John Kennedy?"—was it Oswald alone, was there another bullet, another gun, was Castro involved, was the KGB involved, were the FBI and CIA involved, was Oswald really Oswald?—was a form of collective mourning. So was the controversy clustering around Sirhan Sirhan as Bob's killer.

To raise new theories about the killings was a collective way of reworking and in part undoing them, not letting go of the men, greening their memories. The Kennedy mystique increased, especially in death, and took on a life of its own that not even the Kennedys could deal with.

CHAPTER IV

CHAPPAQUIDDICK: THE SELF-INFLICTED WOUND

1/On His Own: A Confused Search for a Role

2/By the Rude Dyke Bridge

3/Thirteen Puzzles, Three and a Half Hypotheses

4/Camelot and Chappaquiddick: Myth and Countermyth

1

On His Own: A Confused Search for a Role

— 1 —

THE FOURTEEN months between Robert Kennedy's death in June 1968 and the disaster that engulfed Edward Kennedy at Chappaquiddick in August 1969 were as chaotic and impulse-ridden as any in Ted's life until then.

They contain a historic speech, a confused on-again off-again flirtation with a presidential draft movement at the Chicago Convention, an improbable Senate investigative carnival junket to Alaska, some spells of sailing—sometimes grief-shadowed, sometimes boisterous—and a successful but abruptly conceived venture to take over the post of Democratic Senate Whip.

The common element in these activities is that of a lost man trying out various roles for himself in an effort to find one he can live with. It is as if he were trying to put the pieces of his fragmented life together as a grown man, on his own for the first time.

One possibility was to be truly a "Senate man," in a sense in which neither of his brothers had been. But after Bob's death he stayed away from his Senate office, not even dropping by to look at his mail. There is a story of a day when he set out to drive to the Senate building, almost got there—and turned back. There were too many memories and too many people to face.

When he did return he found occasion to make the historic speech in which he likened himself to Bob as the carrier of the

95

family presidential tradition. There was, he said, "no safety in hiding, for any of us." The implication was unavoidable that it was now his duty to pick up the fallen standard and carry it to victory. It was a metaphor that found reverberation. It expressed one strong impulse of Ted's, one direction for him to take, just as withdrawing and pouring his energies into his Senate task expressed another.

Ted threw out these tantalizing morsels either to reveal or becloud his purpose, or more probably they reflected his own utter ambivalence. Much of that summer he seemed to be trying out the role of the private man in love with sailing, almost obsessed with the sea, perhaps hoping to find comfort in its vastness.

A hedonist strain that had always been evident in Ted, even during his most intense griefs, reasserted itself after the first shock of Bob's death. He made no effort to set limits on himself. Fun was what the summer was for—a summer destroyed by death, to be used perhaps to push death into the background.

The stories about the young Senator piled up—about prolonged drinking bouts; about his knack for spotting a pretty girl at a party, breaking in on her partner while dancing, and trying to make off with her; about a raucous drinking bout at an inn with a band of Green Berets, complete with the traditional glass-breaking. At this time in Ted's life, right after Bob's death, the press was kindly, and, except for an occasional story in a picture magazine, few of these accounts found their way beyond the locals and the newsmen to the people at large.

— 2 —

TED did get a lot of attention for a trip, the outgrowth of a promise to his brother Bob, that he organized for a senatorial Subcommittee on Indian Education, to study poverty in Alaska. It was a disaster all around. Ted drank constantly. The photographers and reporters presented the trip as Ted's Alaskan counterpart of his brother's impassioned exploration of Appalachian poverty. Ted played along, basking in his own publicity and finding at least a temporary public role to his liking. The Republican members of the committee pulled out and left for home in protest against the Kennedy media extravaganza. Ted swung between emotional extremes in talking to reporters: At times his mood was shrill, explosive, high, at others uncharacteristically candid about his own fate in the wake of his brothers. ("They'll shoot my ass off the way they did Bobby's.") On the flight home he was drunk, weaving up and down the aisle with cries of "Eskimo Power!"

Somewhat earlier he had shown a mood-swinging volatility on a more important occasion: the chance in reality to raise his brother Bob's fallen standard in a presidential campaign. Understandably Ted was too immersed in shock and grief in June, so soon after the assassination, to pick up on the momentum of Bob's campaign and move on to the convention in his place. By July and August he was more in control, and the national grief and guilt over Bob's killing were still deep enough to offset any charge of opportunism if Ted had moved decisively.

But he did not. Ted made no move of his own, which is to the credit of his sensitivity to what was appropriate, if not of his political drive. He was not Bob, involved with a cause that overrode all other considerations. He was Ted, a bereaved brother and politician, but not an idealist or crusader.

Even as a politican, however, Ted was embroiled in his own mood alternations about running. Mayor Daley of Chicago, Mike DiSalle of Ohio, and a number of Democratic insiders whose weight could be decisive assured him he could have the nomination. They were governed less by idealism than by their own political interest. They despised Eugene McCarthy, liked Hubert Humphrey but mistrusted his capacity to win. They figured—and rightly—that Richard Nixon would be a formidable Republican opponent.

Ted could have given them a graceful, firm, and principled "no." However disappointed, they would have understood it. Or he could have said that he wanted to explore the possibilities, make sure that he was not being played off against McCarthy and Humphrey, and that the convention really wanted him. But he did neither. He sent his brother-in-law, Stephen Smith, to Chicago, to make some soundings—which was taken as an expression of intent. But when McCarthy, while insisting that he wouldn't fight a Ted draft, refused to nominate him Smith returned and the soundings were terminated with extreme prejudice.

In the end Ted said he had never been open to running. If this was true he had played a confusing, pointless game with his supporters. In all probability his tortured course reflected his waxing and waning of purpose as he felt himself torn between his sense of duty to Bob and the dynasty, and his fear of so formidable a testing.*

---

*For a more detailed account of the tangled skein of Ted's motives and attitudes toward the 1968 nomination, see Chapter V, Why Ted Slept: 1968, 1972, 1976. See also the account there of Ted's successful bid for the post of Senate Democratic Whip.

2

By the Rude Dyke Bridge

— 1 —

THE "INCIDENT at Chappaquiddick," which has now entered American history and legendry, started innocently enough with a regatta off Edgartown, on Martha's Vineyard, Massachusetts, July 18, 1969. More than any other event in Ted Kennedy's career it has blocked his path to the White House, called his credibility into question, and damaged the Kennedy legend.

Ted had made a ritual of competing in the regatta every year with his boat *Victura*. In the summers of 1966 and 1967 he seems also to have celebrated the event by a weekend party with friends, involving considerable drinking, gaiety, and whatever else happens at weekend sailing parties. In 1968, so soon after Bob's death, there is no record of Ted in the regatta. But that summer Ted and Joan gave a cocktail party at the Hyannisport compound for the "boiler room girls"—a group of bright, intelligent, and attractive young women who were devoted to Bob and his cause, and had worked hard under great pressure keeping track of delegates and doing other chores in Bob's campaign.

The idea of a 1969 regatta weekend, to which the girls would be invited, came from Joe Gargan, cousin, aide, confidante, drinking companion, and general factotum to Ted. Gargan, orphaned early, had grown up in Ted's family, and Ted found in Joe a constant companion of his own age who was devoted to him and whose existence for years had been given color and substance by the Kennedy family.

Ted, the best sailor of the family, did indifferently in the regatta itself, placing ninth. The members of the party were quartered in several hotels in Edgartown, Ted staying at the small, traditional Shiretown Inn, which he and other Kennedys had often used. By evening the whole party had gathered, by ferry and car, at the Lawrence Cottage, on Chappaquiddick Island, rented for the occasion, remote enough to ensure privacy. Much was made later of the composition of the party—six married men without their wives, and six unmarried women. But the whole group knew each other through their past involvement with Kennedy campaigns, and there was no obvious pairing off among them.

If this was to be a "wild party," in the commonly accepted sense, these seemed to be the wrong women and wrong men for it. The men had in common only the bond of their relationship to Ted. They were: Paul Markham, a lawyer closer to Gargan than to Ted, moving up the political ladder in Massachusetts; Ray LaRosa, a former fireman and a Kennedy hanger-on with a state patronage job; Charles Tretter, another lawyer and Kennedy personal aide; and Ted's aging and hard-drinking driver, Jack Crimmins. These, along with Joe Gargan and Ted, formed a genial, comfortable, but scarcely Dionysian group. The women were young and bright, none of them beauties, most of them attractive: Mary Jo Kopechne, Mary Ellen and Nance Lyons, Rosemary ("Cricket") Keogh, Esther Newburgh, Suzy Tannenbaum: We have seen them, or others like them, working in political headquarters, eager, efficient, resourceful, intelligent, headed for careers.

Not exactly the cast for an orgy, no matter what the private fantasies and the popular imagination later fixed on. Nor does it follow however that the intent was quite as innocent as the cleaned-up version the Kennedy camp was to circulate: that it was just a well-meant effort to reward some girls who had worked hard for Bobby. The likely truth is at once less garish than the popular version and less innocuous than the official one.

There could have been few bacchanalian expectations. One guesses that there was considerable but not heavy drinking. There was a suburban cookout, dragged-out conversation (mostly reminiscences of Bobby's campaign), some dancing, and a little wandering into the mosquito-ridden night. Ted was not his usual life-of-the-party self and—by several reports—didn't seem to be having a very good time.

Up to this point the accounts of the evening are pretty consistent. From this point on there is neither map nor compass. The fact is that, from the time Ted left the party to the time when his car, with Mary Jo's dead body inside, was found by the police, there is little hard evidence. No witnesses to the accident itself have surfaced publicly, and there were very few disinterested witnesses who saw or spoke with Ted.

— 2 —

ON the core events in question, many critics have had a hard time of it because they start with Ted's story, and seek holes, gaps, inconsistencies, and contradictions within it.

What is involved in the whole bundle of basic assumptions that Thomas Kuhn calls the unspoken paradigm, or frame, in scientific experiment or problem solving? If we start with Ted's story in its successive versions, as backed up by several other members of the Lawrence Cottage party in *their* successive versions, we have a question-begging problem: What is in question is the validity of the Kennedy story, and it cannot be settled by using that story as a frame for an answer.

Only if we hold to hard evidence, and ask what hypothesis is most congruent with it, can we hope to approximate what happened. We must therefore treat Ted's own version of the events as one hypothesis to examine and test, for its congruity with the few observed facts—and also with what we know about Ted.

There is much we don't know about the events of the night. Except for Ted's statement as backed up by several of his group, we don't know at what time Ted and Mary Jo left the party, whether they left in Ted's black Oldsmobile together, or even whether they were alone in it. We don't know whether Ted was headed, as he claimed, for the last ferry to Edgartown, to get Mary Jo, or anyone else he was with, to her hotel. We don't know whether he turned off the main road on to the Dyke Road by intent or (as he again claimed) in ignorance of the area. (He had been on both roads several times that day.) We don't know how drunk or sober either of them was, except for an estimate by the medical examiner the next day that Mary Jo had drunk moderately.

We don't know, from the hard evidence of Sheriff "Luck" Look, that he had seen the Oldsmobile being driven down the Dyke Road, had seen two figures in front and something (or someone?) shadowy in the rear, and had jotted down the L's and 7's on the license plate. We don't know whether they stopped anywhere between that point and the bridge. We know the car went over the bridge, but we don't know at what speed, or how, or even who was driving, or whether there was someone else in it other than Mary Joe when it hit the water. We can't even be wholly certain whether Ted was in it at that point.

The answers to our "don't knows" are locked in the knowledge and memory of Senator Edward Kennedy, and he is unlikely ever to tell more than he has already told. Unless there was someone else in the car, the only other person in whose brain the whole story was imprinted was Mary Jo Kopechne, and she will never tell.

Ted's version, now historic, was that he meant to drive to the ferry, took the wrong turn by mistake, had not drunk much, was driving at twenty miles an hour when the car hit the bridge, remembers only the rush of water and the struggle to get out, then the fruitless efforts to dive and rescue Mary Jo against the strong current, his exhaustion, his walk to the cottage, his return to the bridge with Gargan and Markham, their equally fruitless efforts at diving and rescue, their walk to the ferry, where he jumped in and swam across to the mainland, his falling asleep in his room at the inn and being awakened by noise from a party nearby, his brief conversation with the innkeeper (at 2:25 A.M.—Ted asked him for the time), his failure to report the drowning of Mary Jo because of his confusion and a persisting belief that it had not happened and she might still be alive, his waking in the morning, dressing, exchanging some greetings with guests, his meeting with Gargan and Markham, his crossing on the ferry to Chappaquiddick, and being told that the car and girl had been discovered, his return to the mainland, and his statement.

As a commentary on this version there must again be a litany of "don't knows." We don't know what happened to Ted in the car or the water, if indeed he was there. We don't know his thoughts and conversations after the accident, or how much he knew about it. We don't know whether Mary Jo died of drowning or suffocation. We don't know whether Ted dove in the water to rescue Mary Jo, and whether Gargan and Markham helped him later to dive again, nor what Ted and Gargan and Markham discussed that night, nor why his two lawyer friends stayed on at Chappaquiddick when Ted left, nor what they did there. We don't know what the current was like when Ted swam to the mainland, or indeed whether he swam. We don't know what he did with the hours between his appearance at the inn at 2:25 A.M. and his reappearance around eight. We don't know what telephoning was done that night and the next morning, nor by whom and to whom. We don't know whether the statement by Ted to Police Chief Dominick Arena, written down by Markham, never signed by anyone, was composed on the spur of the moment or had been drafted during the night or earlier that morning.

Most of the answers to these "don't knows" are imbedded in Ted's memory, some in the memory of his two lawyer friends, while some may also be known to other members of the party—

perhaps Jack Crimmins, perhaps Rosemary Keogh—who have chosen not to reveal it.

At this point the police and legal system enter, and the process of the administration of law and justice. It is useful to note the succession of phases involving the legal process: the discovery of the car, the diving for Mary Jo's body and its recovery, the assistant medical examiner's hurried examination and his finding of death by drowning, the failure to order an autopsy, the submission of Ted's statement, the quick release of Mary Jo's body for burial, the plea-bargaining meetings, the agreement on the charge, the trial and suspended sentence, the request by District Attorney Dinis for exhuming Mary Jo's body, hearings on it in Pennsylvania, the bungled inquest that raised more questions than it answered because of Judge Boyle's rulings and the exclusion of cross-examination, the stern restrictions by Judge Paquet on a grand jury investigation.

—— 3 ——

MOST of the people involved in the legal process, from local police to the district attorney and the judges, didn't treat Senator Edward Moore Kennedy as they would have treated an obscure tourist on the island who drove away with a girl after a party and turned up, without having reported it to police, the next morning when her dead body was discovered in his car in the pond. In Ted's case they were awed by his office and the Kennedy name, they sensed the high stakes involved, and decided not to do anything that would make things harder for him politically and personally.

They were of course operating under the white light of the media, which poured in on them once the news of the accident was flashed. Nothing comparable had ever happened to this sleepy and serene Vineyard community. Another complicating factor was the contingent of Kennedy familiars—legal and political figures of national importance—who descended on the family compound at Hyannisport, and with whose overpowering presence local officials had also to deal.

Ted had at his command a powerful battery of legal advisers, including a former U.S. Assistant Attorney-General (Burke Marshall) and a prominent New York lawyer (Ted Sorensen) who had been John Kennedy's *alter ego.* He also had a battery of political advisers, among them a former Secretary of Defense (Robert McNamara) and a speech-writer for both John Kennedy and Lyndon Johnson (Richard Goodwin).

It is hard to think of anyone else involved in an accident who was sheathed in such protective layers of legal and political armor, or who had presented the police and court authorities with so formidable a challenge to their good sense and the integrity of their office. Some of them had to summon all their skill and conscience in walking a tightrope between their duty as officials and their concern for their Senator and his family, who were the pride of their small community as well as their state.

Given the whole sequence of the legal and judicial events, it is clear that the Senator was handled not objectively but protectively. The failure to hold an autopsy came out of the refusal of both the medical examiner and the district attorney to take the responsibility for making the decision. Police Chief Dominick Arena, awed by the Senator, waited three hours while the reporters clamored for the release of Ted's statement. He did not even move to charge him until the prosecutor, Walter Steele, told him that the law required it. Two more days passed before Ted's local lawyers called Steele to arrange a plea-bargaining session. It took place secretly, in a hideaway house of Steele's, in order to elude the reporters.

Burke Marshall, sitting with Ted's other advisers, had been concerned about a "driving to endanger" charge or even a manslaughter charge, with their punitive consequences, and counseled Ted, who was eager to get everything over with, against moving too fast. The agreement of the prosecutor to a minor charge of "leaving the scene of the accident," and a suspended prison sentence of two months, got Ted over his legal difficulties exactly in time for the TV broadcast he had scheduled for the evening of the same day, almost exactly a week after the incident itself.

— 4 —

IT had been a terrible week for Ted, the most intense ordeal of his life, and all the worse for being a self-inflicted wound. Coming so soon after Bob's death, it was a shattering experience. In the hour of danger that threatened to pulverize his career, he reached out for support from others.

They came, because the last of the Kennedys needed them. They left whatever they were doing to be at his side. They were mostly Jack's and Bob's associates, and they came because he was the dynastic heir, and, as they still saw it, the carrier of the future of American liberalism.

Ted had phoned his mother at 10:00 A.M. the morning after the accident. She took the news in her fatalistic, supportive way. Later he told his father. The confession ("Dad, I've done the best I can. I'm sorry") must have been hard to utter and hard to hear. It was the patriarch's last blow, and he didn't live long after it.

It isn't clear how much Ted told either his family or his advisers about what really happened. They were using Jacqueline Kennedy's house in the family compound as headquarters and Ted was at his Squaw Island home. He spent most of the week plunged in a dark mood, sailing part of the time, ready to take whatever punishment was meted out to him, ready to leave to the experts the strategy decisions on how to retrieve his all-but-ruined political fortunes.

It was almost as if he had withdrawn himself from the huddle, leaving to the others the responsibility for his rescue, as if he were no longer involved in saving himself. This distancing of himself from his advisers, however necessary emotionally, alienated several of them, who felt that he was not "coming clean" with them, and that he was acting the hurt small boy, not the responsible adult man.

Broadly there were two basic strategies to choose between. One was to tell it pretty much as it was, to let it all "hang out," accept whatever immediate political consequences were likely, and trust that the people would respond to his honesty and manliness. This had its dangers, but if it worked it would get Ted out of the shadow that would otherwise envelop him forever. The other was to shape as reasonable an account as possible, to say nothing incompatible with Ted's statement to the police, and stick with the story at all costs. This too had its dangers, mostly of credibility, but it would save Ted politically, and in the long run —they hoped—he would ride it out.

There were long discussions of segments and details of what would be said. But on the larger question it was the second plan that prevailed. Ted Sorensen did most of the writing. Ted Kennedy himself accepted the overall strategy but insisted on a closing appeal to the people of Massachusetts, written by Milton Gwirtzman, placing Ted and his political future in their hands.

— 5 —

EXACTLY a week after the drowning Ted's family and the advisers gathered at the home of his parents for the talk. Now, with the trial over, the major decisions made, the speech readied, there was the task of delivering it. Ted did it well, as he has generally done his prepared speeches well. When he was finished the family had dinner together, then Ted excused himself and went back to Squaw Island.

Across the nation a vast, stunned audience listened to the youngest Kennedy son tell the painful, bedraggled, almost unbelievable story. No one who heard it at the time is likely to forget its carefully constructed segments as it guided the listener, step by step, past the pitfalls of circumstance, across the abysses of character, to the safe harbor of Ted's contrition and his submission to the verdict of the people of Massachusetts themselves.

The speech was bound to prove a straitjacket governing Ted's utterances on the subject ever since. The basic themes to which he clings were all there: that the island cookout was innocent, that his attentions to Mary Jo—"a gentle, kind and idealistic person" —were to "help her feel that she still had a home with the Kennedy family," that there was no "immoral conduct" between them, that he was not "driving under the influence of liquor," that they left the party at 11:15 P.M., that he almost drowned in his efforts to rescue Mary Jo, that he suffered a "cerebral concussion as well as shock," that it was "indefensible" of him not to report the accident, that he was in a state of "physical, emotional trauma" that could account for "the various inexplicable, inconsistent and inconclusive things I said and did," that the question whether "the girl might still be alive somewhere out of that immediate area" and "whether some awful curse did actually hang over the Kennedys" and "whether somehow the awful weight of this incredible incident might in some way pass from my shoulders" all went through his mind, and that he was "overcome by a jumble of emotions—grief, fear, doubt, exhaustion, panic, confusion and shock."

There followed his account of going to the ferry with Gargan and Markham, jumping into the water on an impulse, collapsing in his room about 2 A.M., going out "at one point" to talk to the room clerk, being "somewhat more lucid" in the morning, phoning Burke Marshall and "belatedly" reporting the accident.

There followed also his contrition: that he felt "morally obligated" to plead guilty to the charge of leaving the scene, that he felt "pain and suffering" and "grief," and that he wondered whether his "standing among the people" had been "so impaired" that he should resign his Senate seat.

He invoked the great names of past Massachusetts Senators

—John Quincy Adams, Daniel Webster, Charles Sumner, Henry Cabot Lodge, John Kennedy—as evidence that he would have to "inspire" the "utmost confidence" of the people, reminded his listeners that his seven years in the Senate contained "glorious" as well as "very sad" memories, and asked for their "advice and opinion" and their "prayers" to help him with the decision he would have to make "on my own." It would require "courage," not by summoning "stories of past courage" but by "looking into his own soul." He ended by the hope that he could "put this most recent tragedy behind me" and go on contributing "to our state and mankind."

— 6 —

IN its own way the speech was a masterpiece of evasions, half-truths, omissions, elisions, shadings of meaning, and appeals to emotion, all contributing to form a mawkish piece of special pleading rather than the bare and honest narrative of events that was called for, and a manful assumption of responsibility.

The first reaction to the speech was overwhelmingly favorable, with a storm of telegrams and a wave of compassion for Ted's plight, admiration for his courage, and support for his remaining in office. In immediate impact the strategy of Ted's advisers paid off.

In long-range terms it was a disaster. The nation didn't feel about the speech as Boston and Massachusetts did. The second wave of opinion condemned it as a compact of "cheapness and bathos," as "hustling heartstrings," and as "a cold, heartless, political maneuver."

What Ted's political fate and mental resolution might have been if he had insisted on total candor in the speech—the road not taken—we cannot know. But it could scarcely be worse than what happened. Someone else had written the words and music that

Ted sang at his father's house, on that night of July 25, 1969, while the old man sat upstairs closed off from the enactment below, helpless to control or even influence the history that was being made that night.

Five days later, after the avalanche of supportive letters and wires, Ted announced that he would remain in the Senate. The next day, July 31, he told the media that he would not be a presidential candidate for the 1972 election. Evidently he was happy to have his Senate career salvaged and secure, and the gesture of renunciation of higher things was not lost on the voters.

It was on November 18, 1969, four months after the night of Chappaquiddick, that Joseph P. Kennedy died. He had been ailing ever since the episode, and there were those who wondered whether he still had the will to live. His only surviving son, Ted, spent that last night next to his father's bed, rolled up in a sleeping bag.

3

Thirteen Puzzles, Three and a Half Hypotheses

— 1 —

PART OF THE legacy of Chappaquiddick that we have all inherited is a bundle of puzzles. Some of them have been the subject of discussion in mountains of articles and books. I present them summarily, in rough chronological order:

1. *Timing.* Ted's story is that he left the cottage with Mary Jo around 11:15, to make the ferry to the mainland. The last one was scheduled to leave at midnight, although there was a sign saying the ferry could be summoned, by bell or headlights, at any hour. Sheriff Christopher ("Luck") Look's testimony that he saw Ted's car at 12:45 on Dyke Road and noted portions of its license plate is a hard bit of evidence against Ted's story. Ted's insistence on the 11:15 time makes sense only if he meant to hide his intent to drive to the beach, not the ferry.

2. *The turnoff on Dyke Road.* Ted maintains that he made the turn in ignorance of the road. There is strong evidence that he had in fact been on the road several times earlier that day. There is strong evidence that it would be hard to mistake the difference once one made the turn. Judge Boyle, after the inquest, was emphatic about Ted's intent to make the turnoff.

3. *Driving speed.* Ted said he was driving twenty m.p.h. over the bridge. Judge Boyle considered even that speed "negligent and reckless." A technical study commissioned by the *Readers' Digest*

111

calculates that Ted had to be driving from thirty to thirty-eight m.p.h. to plunge from the bridge. Ted's friends knew him to be a reckless, self-destructive driver and often expressed anxiety about it. Ted's insistence makes sense only if he feared a manslaughter charge for reckless driving.

4. *Sober or drunk?* Ted insists that he was not intoxicated that night. This is possible but scarcely probable. He was known to be a heavy party drinker, and there was no reason to break the pattern, even if the party was dull—especially if it had been dull. No breath test was given Ted, whatever it might have shown after an overnight sleep. Mary Jo would have known, but she died.

5. *Getting out, rescue attempts.* Ted's account of getting out of the car is understandably vague. He spoke of the rush of water and of pummeling by Mary Jo. He would have had to get out either through the rolled-down window on his side or the two blown-out windows at Mary Jo's. She was small and slight, he massive. It should have been easier for her to get out than for him to squeeze his bulk through. The difference was his greater strength. Once out of the car even a strong swimmer, like Ted, could have had a hard time getting Mary Jo out, although his account of the strong tide and currents that night has been called in question by the *Readers' Digest* study.

6. *Getting help.* This is a crucial, heartbreaking puzzle. Exhausted and confused as Ted must have been, by his version, why didn't he get immediate help, once his rescue efforts had failed? There was a house with a light four hundred feet from the bridge, and a fire station with a phone visible from the dirt road. Ted said later he was convinced the girl was dead. It was a fearful conclusion to make on his own. Besides, if he felt that, why did he then —by his version—return with his two friends for further rescue efforts?

7. *Keeping them in the dark.* When Ted did get back to Lawrence Cottage, why didn't he spread the alarm about the drowned or drowning girl, not only to his two close lawyer friends but to the other nine members of the party? Gargan and Markham

later said they didn't want to "alarm" the girls, and gave them confusing and bizarre reports about Mary Jo being in her room at the inn, or in a car stuck on the road, or (next morning) in an "accident." Why the mystery? There were three able-bodied men (one, Raymond LaRosa, a fireman trained in scuba-diving rescue) and five women whose help could have been enlisted and wasn't. It is hard to escape the conclusion that the trio was less interested in saving Mary Jo's life than in saving Ted's career.

8. *The second rescue effort.* Ted's story in his TV speech— and also that of Gargan and Markham at the inquest—was that all three returned to the bridge for rescue efforts. But neither Ted nor they mentioned it when Ted made his statement to the police. There might have been a way of checking their account if there had been cross-examination. Lacking that, we are in the dark about what the three men actually said and did that night. No one reported seeing them wet when they returned to the cottage. Ted's account that Gargan's arm was "scraped . . . bruised and bloodied" is puzzling because Arena saw him the next day in short sleeves and noted nothing, nor did his friends according to their testimony in the inquest.

9. *Failure to notify.* After the second rescue attempt—if indeed it was made—the moral as well as legal responsibility to notify the police became all the heavier. Ted did not call the police, and his friends say they didn't because they counted on him, and they also fell back on a client-lawyer relationship, which seems a flimsy explanation.

Ted said later his failure to notify was "indefensible," and blamed it on his persisting hopes and delusions that he would wake up and find her alive somewhere. But he failed to report it even after he awoke, and postponed it for several hours more, until he crossed back to Chappaquiddick and heard at the ferry that the car and girl had been found. Ted's later statement that this was "indefensible" doesn't make it any less the deepest puzzle of all.

10. *Across the channel and into the inn.* Ted said he asked his friends to take him to the ferry so he could get back to the

mainland. He could have rung for a ferry, even that late, but evidently did not. How "impulsive," as he later put it, could his plunge into the channel have been—if indeed he made it? His account that there were "heavy tides" has been challenged since, in a controversy of experts over tide tables and changes of currents. Even if the current were less adverse than he later said, it would still have been a trying swim. But except as adding another item to the credibility problem, this isn't crucial.

Once across, and presumably into his bed at the inn, his appearance at 2:25 A.M.—dressed, asking the innkeeper the time, complaining about noise from a party—is peculiar, except as an effort to establish his presence at that time. Even more so was his unruffled behavior at 7:15 and 8:30 in amiable conversations with the regatta winner at breakfast and later in ordering the newspapers. At 9 A.M., getting on the ferry with Gargan and Markham, and at 9:30—first told about the discovery of the car and girl— he gave no indication of his own involvement. It was only when another ferry captain told him again about the dead girl at 9:45 that Ted said, "Yes, I know," and rode back to the mainland and the police. This was either a man of iron control, keeping his counsel with a cold detachment, or acting out a role in a fashion strangely incongruent with his scenario of what had happened at the bridge or inside his mind.

11. *The puzzle of the "Yes."* When Chief Arena asked him if there were any other passengers in the car with him, Ted answered "Yes." Asked later whether there was anyone else in the water he said "No." The first answer could have been a confused "Yes" to a misunderstood question, but still a puzzle, which bears on an alternate hypothesis I shall be discussing, of the presence of another girl in the car.

12. *The mystery of the missing phone call lists.* The company records of phone calls made by Ted or on his credit cards were obviously of crucial importance. They were not subpoenaed until the inquest. But for a number of reasons nothing came of it. The subpoena never reached the Chesapeake and Potomac Company, and was never followed up. When the New England Telephone

Company officials brought four lists of calls to court, the examining assistant district attorney, Armand Fernandes, introduced only one into evidence and never asked about the others, which were never volunteered.

There were a number of intra-company discussions about the records but none was either queried or revealed. The list introduced showed sixteen calls from Martha's Vineyard, of which the earliest was at 7:52 A.M., to a woman associate of Ted's brother-in-law, Stephen Smith, who was traveling in Europe. An article in the Manchester *Union Leader,* a strongly anti-Kennedy paper, on August 13, 1969, said seventeen calls had been made "in the middle of the night after the accident." It was presumably based on company records leaked by an employee. The unexamined lists have been since destroyed.

The New York Times did a full investigatory account of the mystery of the phone records on March 12, 1980. Ted made an indignant response to the *Times* article, calling it, like other inquiries, an intrusion into the privacy of "my life, the life of my wife, my children, my nieces and nephews." It remains true however that the complete records could be of great importance in shedding light on whether Ted and his associates had—as the *Times* writers put it—"the presence of mind to make telephone calls during the 10-hour delay" when Ted described himself as "in a state of confusion and shock," unable to report the accident.

13. *Could Mary Jo have been saved?* It isn't at all certain, despite the original guess of the assistant medical examiner, that she died from drowning. The diver found her in a position where she seemed to be trying to breathe air trapped in a bubble at the footwell of the car where the water level didn't totally fill it. He guessed that she might have lived for several hours after the accident. The mortician said her body looked as if she had died of suffocation rather than drowning. The lack of an autopsy makes it impossible for us ever to know.

— 2 —

THESE thirteen puzzles are not discrete items. They form an interconnecting pattern. Each presents a gap in our information about what happened, within the frame of the Ted-Gargan-Markham account. But any explanation that would fill several of these gaps might fill others as well.

This has led to the floating of a number of theories or hypotheses that might explain what happened. I regard the Kennedy-Gargan-Markham version as one hypothesis, and have largely rejected it as a leaky one.

A second has been suggested by a number of people, most notably in Jack Olsen's book, *The Bridge at Chappaquiddick*. It has Ted leaving the car after it was spotted by Sheriff Look, to hide on the side of the road while Mary Jo drove on to the bridge alone. The idea was that Ted, fearful that Look might investigate further, didn't want to take a chance at discovery. If Look left them alone, Mary Jo could pick him up again in a few minutes.

The merit of this hypothesis is that it would better explain how the car, with a slight woman at the wheel, who had never driven it before, could have gone off the bridge. Even more, it would explain why Ted and his friends—uncertain whether Mary Jo was alive or dead, uncertain even that the car was in the water—would delay reporting the accident, debate about what to do, spend the night waiting for a miracle that didn't come, and move into action only when the car and girl were discovered.

Two things are hard to accept in this hypothesis. One is the initial assumption of a Ted so scared by passing the sheriff's car that he would get out, hide, and send Mary Jo on. At that point he had nothing to run from. The second is the assumption that Ted, when he learned the next morning that Mary Jo was dead, would concoct the story of having been in the car with her and driven her to her death. Even if his primary motivation were to save his career, he would be endangering it far more by his story than by the reality.

A third hypothesis is the widely bruited one of a "second woman" who was in the car with Ted and Mary Jo. There had been earlier speculations about it. But Ladislas Farago, in a paperback, *Worse than a Crime*—in press as I write—has used FBI records and other fresh material to flesh it out.

The Farago hypothesis suggests the following scenario: that Ted left the party for the mainland with Rosemary Keogh, leaving behind his driver, Jack Crimmins—who had drunk a little too much; that Crimmins knew that Mary Jo was in the back seat, sleeping off her drinking and her earlier exposure to the sun, but forgot to warn Ted; that they drove off, found themselves somehow on the Dyke Road, whether by a wrong turn or by intent; that when Ted got out near the bridge, to stretch or for whatever other reason, Rosemary—in some dudgeon—drove onto the bridge, tried to turn around, and drove into the pond; that she managed to get out, swim back and join Ted; that the two returned to the cottage, where Crimmins told them about the sleeping girl; that Ted, Gargan and Markham then addressed themselves to the problem of how Ted could extricate himself from his involvement; that Crimmins, penitent about his failure to warn Ted about Mary Jo, later meant to go to Chief Arena with his account but was frightened off by the array of reporters.

I find this hypothesis unsatisfactory too. It is ingenious, and does answer several otherwise unexplained puzzles: why Ted said "Yes" to Arena's question about "another person" in the car, why Rosemary's bag was found in the car by the police, why Joe Gargan told the people at the cottage that Mary Jo was missing and couldn't be found.

But it runs afoul of any rational calculation of Ted's motives and conduct after the accident. Why would he, in the account he gave the police, place himself in the car when he wasn't there? Surely his public image as squiring two women in an auto ride at night was no worse and probably more acceptable than if he had gone off into the night with one. The whole effort at concocting a cover story more tortured, and more culpable, than the true one, makes little sense.

— 3 —

IN sifting these hypotheses, including Ted's, the central fact we start with is his state of mind. In his TV speech he emphasized the "fear" and "panic" that engulfed him that night. They were at the center of the storm in the medley of emotions in his mind. Yet whether he thought Mary Jo was dead, or hoped against hope that she wasn't, everything indicates that his preoccupation was not with the death and his measure of responsibility but with how the world would perceive it and what it would mean for his political career.

Those who have studied Chappaquiddick have been so absorbed with the inconsistencies and gaps in Ted's story that they have lost sight of what counts. With so many gaps in what he said he did, it is better to start with his state of mind and emotions and use it to reconstruct his actions.

The "fear" and "panic" he felt were not over his physical but his political survival. He had lived through the Harvard exam scare and the Virginia police scare, both of which endangered whatever career lay ahead of him. But now he was on his own, confronting starkly the possible wreck of his career if the story of the night at Dyke Bridge got out.

This became the continuing theme: not to let "it" become public, whatever "it" was. If this is so, it gives us at least one warning—to reject a hypothesis involving a set of actions that would put him in a better light than in the account he chose to narrate. This is the crucial reason why I am skeptical about the "Teddy wasn't at the wheel" and the "second woman" hypotheses. Both versions, however ingenious, mitigate both his responsibility and his guilt. I should hazard that Ted was too good a driver to go off the bridge unless he were driving fast and had drunk too much. His denials are understandable, given his concern about his career, and the possibility of opening himself to a manslaughter charge.

This doesn't answer the critical question of Ted's failure to call immediately for help when it might have saved Mary Jo's life. It carries a heavier moral burden than anything he may have done, including drinking, speeding, and dumping his Oldsmobile in Pousha Pond. How explain it? I accept his having somehow extricated himself and struggled to the surface after the plunge. I am willing to assume his efforts to dive for the girl without success, and his confused walk to the cottage. I am very skeptical, however, of the effort of Gargan and Markham to dive for the girl again. It was not in Ted's original statement nor the one he made at the trial, and has the feel of an afterthought. It would be a necessary afterthought to answer the charge of heartlessness in failing either to report the drowning or to summon help.

Thus the only way to explain the failure to call help or report the accident is to assume in Ted's mental state a mix of fear, fantasy, and hope—fear of the consequences for his career, fantasy in his incapacity to act and his paralysis of will, hope, a delusive, crazy hope, that the girl might somehow have escaped and survived.

All three might combine to make him delay, fearing disclosure, helpless to act because of his fear, rationalizing it by his fantasy hope, hiding from the reality principle as he had hidden at every crisis of his life by turning over to his father and brothers the task of coping with reality.

That night many strands from his past may have come together to augment and distort the reality of the disaster he faced in the present. Old anxieties as to his adequacy, premonitions of failure, habits of dependency, evoked once again the flight pattern that marked his response to other, less crucial episodes in his past. In this crisis, alone for the first time to face an episode that could destroy him, he acted as his life development up to that time had shaped him to act.

4

Camelot and Chappaquiddick: Myth and Countermyth

— 1 —

WHAT HAPPENED to Ted at Chappaquiddick could have happened to anyone. So we have repeatedly been told, but there are many who wonder. In any event what counted was his response to it. What happened to Ted was in part a matter of chance, while Ted's response was a matter of character. It was his character, engraved in him by the circumstance of his biography, that shaped his action, in what he did and failed to do, in taking shelter in fantasy instead of facing reality with a measure of courage and decisiveness.

Once Mary Jo's body had been found and Ted had made his statement to police, he was surrounded by his lawyers, advisers, and family aides, and he reverted to his old, familiar pattern of reality. Everything could be controlled now. He gave a selective account of the accident to Police Chief Arena. His lawyers, with the help of the police, the prosecutor, and several judges, managed to steer him through the rocks and shoals of the justice system of the state. The district attorney's office muffed the chance to question the Kennedy group and the island people early on, and later, when Kennedy had been given his suspended sentence, it was too late. As a result the inquest, when it came, did not allow for cross-examination and adversary procedures. The grand jury foreman, a young islander who was deeply troubled by the prevailing climate of collaboration and the imposed silence, was kept by a political judge from moving into the case.

Thus nothing was permitted to disturb the polished surface of Ted's TV apologia. The whole power of the legal system was invoked, not to uncover the truth of what happened but to buffer Ted with protection against any too zealous investigation of the truth. Ted's lawyers and advisers were skillful in making use of this protective police and judicial armor, but it must be added that it was there and willing to be used.

If this was not "stonewalling" or a "cover-up" in the Watergate sense, there were nonetheless those elements on the side of the Kennedy camp who revealed as little as they had to as selectively as they could, and clammed up on the rest.

There was no application of the principle of equality before the law. Instead a double standard was used. Ted, as a Senator breaking the law, not only got better treatment than some unknown offender might have received, he got far better treatment than many public officials who have run afoul of the law and tried to cover up in order to save their careers. If there had been a Judge Sirica in the Kennedy case, as there was in the later case of Richard Nixon, to use the full power of his judicial office to break down the intimate little network of Ted and his Rosencrantz and Guildenstern, and get beyond their story to the bedrock reality, the result would have been very different. Instead there were complacency and collusion by most of the authorities, until Ted's story was safely shielded from further digging, and protected by his legal rights.

At that point Ted was himself imprisoned in his own story, for good. Once he had established its basic outline and made his TV speech and given his answers to the questions in the inquest, he had no leeway ever again to retrace or amend or retract. Even the filling-in of details became taboo, on the principle that if you respond to a raindrop and a gust of wind, you invoke the storm.

Thus it became, politically and psychologically, not only an understandable tactic but a necessary one. Having made his basic choice of strategy Ted had no later choice except to stonewall it with his formula answer about how "indefensible" his conduct had been and how he had to live with it, and how "that's how it was."

— 2 —

THE real choice came much earlier. After the selective statement to the police, Ted might still have chosen at the time of the TV speech to let the full story emerge. He didn't, for reasons that must have struck him and his advisers as expedient, or smart or both.

But the expedient may not be prudent, and the smart is not always wise. This is not the long debated question of morality in political decision—an area where Ted has a good record. Nor is it the equally debated question of candor about a politician's private life. Like the rest of us, a political figure has the right of privacy, unless he gets into trouble with the law, or unless his private life is turned, by his own conduct, into a valid political issue of character.

The question with Ted is neither about his guile in public policy nor his conduct in private life. It turns on an episode that became at once legal and moral, and which was handled sleazily on both counts—as John Gregory Dunne has put it in his piece in *New West*—to "diminish us all." A choice by Ted Kennedy, for candor against guile, for honesty against cleverness, and for responsibility against a pious acceptance of blame, could once have been made. It can no longer without opening floodgates that could sweep Ted out of even his safe Senate seat.

Which means that in the process of saving himself from the immediate dangers of an open and serious Chappaquiddick trial, and perhaps the loss of the 1970 Senate election, Ted became a prisoner of the story he could no longer change, and whose unanswered questions and puzzles have survived in the public memory and returned again and again to haunt him. He had purchased political survival by the adroit manipulation of legal technicalities that spared him the consequences of cross-examination and a grand jury probe. But by that fact a kind of death-in-life rigidity has kept the Chappaquiddick issue morbidly alive, and prevented any true moral or political closure.

— **3** —

THUS has been born a Chappaquiddick myth, in the sense of a larger-than-life story that everyone has a theory about and offers a solution for. Chappaquiddick was tragic, as were the assassinations. But Chappaquiddick was also sordid. It brought into question Ted's courage, gallantry, core manliness, and his capacity to think and act in a crisis. And these questions were at odds with the quintessential Kennedy family myth, with its elements of grace, power, wit, bravery, irresistible success, and a legendary potency that matched whatever demands were made on a Kennedy. None of these elements, except for the shabby manipulations of family power, is present in the Chappaquiddick myth. Not even the idea of tragic destiny is present, despite Ted's strained effort in his TV speech to invoke the idea of a "family curse."

One can understand why the thought occurred to him. The idea of a family curse is the shadow side of the Kennedy cult of a special family destiny, as Chappaquiddick is the dark and "other" side of Camelot, a countermyth to the shining myth of Camelot. But where the past tragedies could be seen as Fate afflicting the Kennedys, at Chappaquiddick it was not some mysterious Fate but a very real Ted Kennedy who was responsible. It was not a Kennedy who died but an innocent—Mary Jo Kopechne—and her death could not be foisted off on a mystical source that would not have to face either law or conscience.

Chappaquiddick could have remained a pathetic accidental death, a seven-day wonder in the media. It was Ted himself who, for all his repeated efforts at a closure of Chappaquiddick, evoked the countermyth. He knows that his most reliable support is the halo effect of the Camelot myth, which became attached to Jack after his death and then came to include his whole tenure. He also knows that the Chappaquiddick myth can blot out the other, happier Camelot image. It saps his strength in two ways: by undercutting his Camelot support and by bringing into question his own character and capacity. For both reasons he has had to deny it and fight it, and it has in turn played havoc with him.

—— 4 ——

IN certain ways Chappaquiddick may have been a learning experience for Ted. It taught him how strong the popular feeling still is about its perception of personal conduct, and how serious was his loss of the image of a golden boy with a picture-book wife and children.

One way to counter Chappaquiddick was to talk about expiation. Arthur Schlesinger, who has known Ted for years, said just before the 1980 campaign that all Ted's life since Chappaquiddick was a "continuing expiation." It may well be so, since it is hard for anyone except Ted himself to know how much guilt he has actually carried, and how much he has changed as a result. We can only get indirect hints of it from the evidence of his life. But expiation would require something other than his continued refusal to tell the whole Chappaquiddick story.

More than expiation, the test of Chappaquiddick as a learning experience for Ted must be character. Schlesinger has said that with Chappaquiddick "the iron entered Ted's soul." Whether it did or not can only be determined by following his continuing line of conduct in the past decade and now, and its expression in public and private life. We turn to this in the chapters that follow, on Ted as Senator and as presidential contender, as legend and as man.

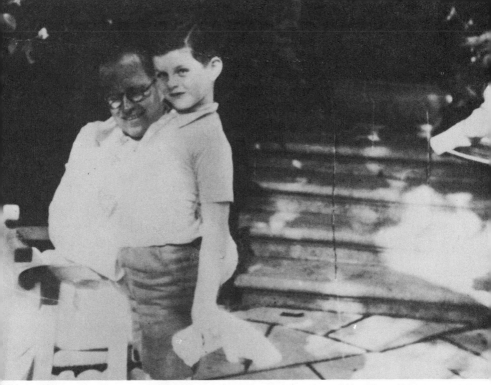

Ted and Joe Sr.: The Patriarch and the Late-Born.

Ted and Joe Jr.: Ted with his first Brother/Father.

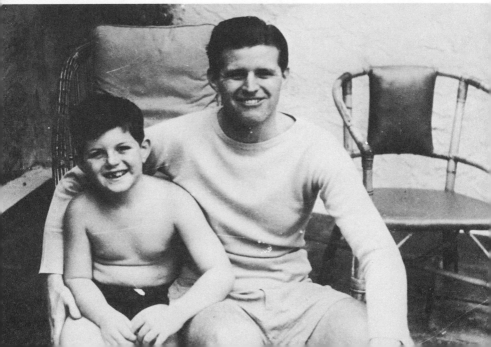

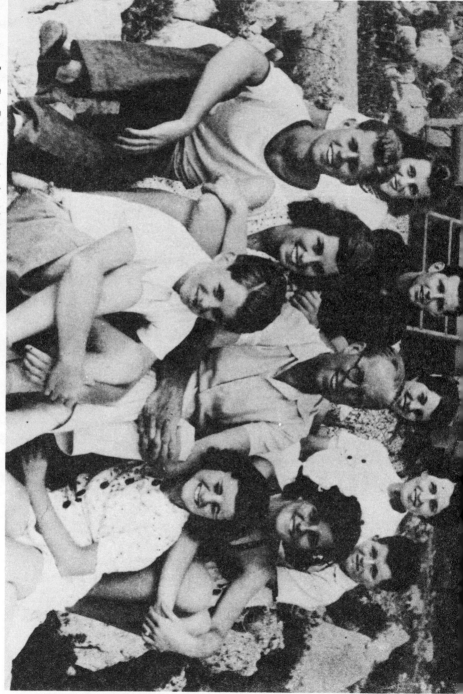

Joe Sr., Rose, and their children: The closeness and fierce complicity of the Kennedy family.

Band of Brothers

Ted and his family:
Intimacy Relations
From left, Joan, Kara, Ted,
Ted Jr., and Patrick.

"I had made up my mind to raise
my children as perfectly as possible."

It couldn't have been a cordial conversation.

CHAPTER V

SENATE HARBOR, PRESIDENTIAL SEA

1/The Good Senator

2/Intimacy Relations

3/Why Ted Slept: 1968, 1972, 1976

1

The Good Senator

— 1 —

A MIDST the wrack and turbulence of Ted's adult life it is the Senate that has furnished the element of continuity. It has been the steadying force for him, the harbor to which he returned after every scarring experience.

Most of Ted's critics agree that he has been a good, if not great, Senator—so good many think that he ought to live out his public career in the Senate, instead of aiming at the Presidency. What is implied is that, by mind, temperament and character, he is suited to the one, not the other. The thesis is worth examining.

At present writing (1980) Ted has been a Senator for seventeen years. Yet he is still not typed as a Senator but as a Kennedy. Being a Senator, however, within his particular frame of personality and character, makes him the distinctive Kennedy he is.

There are a number of skills involved in the political vocation —those of campaigner, legislator, administrator, decision-maker —that don't always go together. What they have in common is a drive to power, a skill in maneuver, a capacity to relate to the people in sensing and expressing their life needs. Ted has some of those skills, not others.

It was a happy accident that Ted became a legislator, which was where his talents mainly lay. When his father thought about his future he was right to think of a post connected with the home base in Massachusetts, where his own influence would count. And he was right to discard the idea of the Governorship, and not only for reasons of local politics. It would not have suited Ted, who is no administrator, and might have made only a middling Governor. Boston, moreover, was too far from the Washington power center and the action and excitement he craved.

Neither Jack Kennedy nor Bob was ever truly a legislator. They passed through the turnstile, but their hearts were in other things. Despite his years in Congress, Jack thought in large strategic presidential terms, and Bob was an investigator and scrapper. Ted was better fitted for the Senate than either. He enjoyed the four campaigns he waged, was good with his constituents, genial and tactful with his colleagues, effective at committee hearings. He assembled a good staff, was responsive to their briefings, liked the substantive and procedural problems that legislative issues carried with them, and used the debating and moot court skills acquired at college and law school. He could deliver a speech well, and handle a press conference so long as the questions were focused on the programs and politics he knew. In short, from 1963 until today he has been where he belongs.

Given his path to the Senate, at thirty, by way of his brother's power and his father's maneuvers, he was careful to watch his manners and defer to his seniors for a long stretch. He waited fifteen months, until April 1964, before delivering his maiden speech, too late for his brother Jack to hear it or to counsel him. The theme he chose was central to the time: the civil rights cause that Jack cared deeply about and Bob was continuing to fight for. The bill he championed was not popular with his Massachusetts constituents, but Ted has never lacked political courage.

In the speech he linked black rights with past struggles against discrimination by Catholics, Irish, and Jews. He agreed that prejudice is deeply based in man, but appealed to the "noble characteristic" of fairness and good will, which "wants to come out." He ended with his slain brother Jack whose "heart and soul are in the bill." "If his life and death had a meaning, it was that we should not hate but love one another." Thus his first Senate speech established a basic pattern that was to serve him well—to take an advanced liberal position, to admit the difficulties in it, to state the benefits that overbalance them, and to conclude with an appeal to the better angels of our nature.

There followed a succession of Kennedy speeches, bills, and positions: on the Southern poll tax, on civil voting rights, on one-man-one-vote reapportionment, on the draft, on antipoverty programs and model cities, on neighborhood health centers, on the teacher corps, on refugees, on the immigration laws, on the Vietnam War, on defense systems and costs, on the economy, on health care, on a redrafting of the criminal code. There is scarcely anything in the whole range of national policy that he has not touched, and applied to it the liberal positions he derived from all the sources, familial and political, that shaped his view.

— **2** —

ONE source was the Irish and immigrant heritage of the Kennedys, which predisposed them to liberal Democratic doctrine. A second was the New Deal tradition of Franklin Roosevelt that his brother Jack adopted and adapted, with its activist view of the need for federal intervention in the economy and society.

After Jack's death Ted came strongly, as we have seen, under Bob's influence, as Bob himself turned in a radical Populist direction. The important new emphasis came on two issues. One was greater militancy on ethnic rights (as with the Puerto Ricans and the Chicanos) on the model of black civil rights. The other was a movement away from Jack Kennedy's containment of Soviet expansion, toward a far-reaching anti-interventionist position. This involved a corollary movement away from Jack's stress on the defense and intelligence services (note Jack's "missile gap" attack on the Eisenhower Administration) to a reliance on détente diplomacy and a stern opposition to heavier defense expenditures.

In this respect Ted seemed to be returning in part to his father's isolationist stand.

A third source of Ted's Senate positions has been the liberal intellectual community, especially Harvard and M.I.T., in Cambridge. The liberal wing of the Democrats, since Woodrow Wilson, has traditionally drawn on university faculty for support and recruiting, moving away from the rural Midwestern and Southern Populism of the turn of the century, to the largely urban and Eastern upper-middle New Class, of which the universities form the intellectual support grid. John Kennedy, following FDR's "Brain Trust" as a model, almost depopulated the Harvard and M.I.T. faculties by his recruiting from them. Bob had similar university ties for his policy positions.

Ted's links with these groups, as Senator from Massachusetts, were understandably even closer. After a shaky start in his 1962 campaign, when a number of academics felt outraged at the hubris of his candidacy, he cemented his ties with them, even (as I have noted) from his hospital bed after his air crash. After Bob's death, when he had to formulate his Senate positions alone, he continued to take his lead from the Cambridge group, with whom he felt increasingly at home and who in turn got their power leverage from him.

On inflation and income policies, on price, profits and interest controls, on energy programs, on tax reform, on regulation and deregulation, on corporate concentration, on environmental protection and urban plight, on unemployment among black youth, on health-care programs, on detente and SALT, on nonmilitary aid to Third World nations, on enforcing human rights standards even in the case of allies, on deemphasizing the intelligence services, on crime and punishment, on civil liberties and censorship, on the revision and codification of criminal law, on military spending, on the ABM and the neutron bomb and the MX-missile and other weapons programs—on the whole range of issues that engaged Ted as Senator in the years since Bob's death, he got his original marching orders from his father and brothers, and his current social philosophy as well as his targets, tactics, and ammunition from the liberal intellectuals of the New Class.

He expressed as constantly as any long-term Senate member of either party the traditional liberalism of the New Deal, carried over from the thirties and forties into the sixties and seventies. It is the economics, politics, sociology, and philosophy of the welfare state and welfare society.

Its economic assumption is that a market economy is at the mercy of greed and anarchy and cannot operate fairly or effectively except within the frame of state regulation and control. Its power assumption is that concentrated corporate power is a greater menace to freedom than concentrated state power. Its assumption about the relation of man and state is basically collectivist—that the individual must be supported and protected by the state, and that the Constitution guarantees him life, liberty, and the pursuit of entitlements. Its legal premise is based on rights rather than duties, and its social premise on the differing claims of class, group, and ethnic interests rather than on the web of interconnectedness in the social contract beyond the bounds of these social divisions.

Its theory of human nature is one of man's perfectibility, its values system stresses personal fulfillment rather than a work, incentives, and achievement system, its educational theory is permissive, its ethic relativist, its intimacy system diffused, its metaphysic of rights absolutist, its theology a perpetual battle between the angels of light and the forces of darkness.

— 3 —

TED has never made this explicit, perhaps not even to himself. He is not a philosophic man, and perhaps not even aware of his own premises or of the underlying assumptions of the liberal welfare society to which he is committed. Perhaps that is one reason why he has been able to embrace it so fully, without asking whether its premises are still viable, or how great are its costs for the individual and society.

Ted's importance as Senator rests not only on the range, number, and impact of his bills and votes but on his own symbolic character. He is the very perfect model of the liberal Senator. No other liberal Democrat—not Gaylord Nelson of Minnesota nor Birch Bayh of Indiana nor Alan Cranston of California, not even George McGovern of North Dakota—can match the monolithic liberalism of Senator Kennedy of Massachusetts. His liberalism rating for his voting record by the Americans for Democratic Action was consistently 100 on a scale of 100, and only in the last two years did it fall to 98. His conservatism rating by the American Conservative Union has been one (1).

How explain so sustained a record over a span of seventeen years? The Kennedy family tradition is doubtless part of it. But Joe Kennedy was scarcely a liberal, although he thought liberalism a useful platform for his sons. Jack Kennedy rethought the premises of FDR's liberalism and Adlai Stevenson's, and fashioned his own brand, especially on foreign policy, which led many of the faithful to doubt his credentials.

Nor can we say, studying Ted's speeches, that the key to his liberalism is ideology. Bob was more of an ideologue than Ted. The key to Ted's political attitudes is, I suspect, more historical than ideological. In shaping his early views he followed Jack closley during Jack's Senate years, and as Senator himself during the brief period after Ted's first election, before Jack was shot. After his 1964 election to a full term, until Bob's death in 1968, he worked to sort out Jack's brand of liberalism and Bob's, with Bob's influence gaining from year to year as Bob and he shed the layers of Jack's influence. It was on foreign policy that the differences were greatest. Ted and Bob moved away from Jack on aid to friendly but "flawed" nations (flawed by repressive regimes), on counterinsurgency operations in Latin America, on the Cold War with Russia and China, on the Vietnam War itself. It was the inner debate on the battlefield of Ted's mind between the stands of Jack and Bob, which may explain why his support of the war lingered after Bob's, and why he didn't break with Lyndon Johnson until very late in the war.

Ted's relations with Lyndon Johnson were less abrasive than Bob's, but no Kennedy liked Johnson, and once Ted had rounded the decisive point of opposing the war his dislike of Johnson—present and in retrospect—hardened his liberal anti-war position. This proved even truer of his feelings about Richard Nixon, who was the Prince of Darkness for the Kennedy brothers. For eleven out of his eighteen years in the Senate, Ted served under the Presidency of the two men whom he and his family despised. His feeling was more tolerant of Gerald Ford, with whom he worked amicably for the SALT negotiations and the thawing out of the Cold War with China and Russia. But Jimmy Carter in the White House was little more to Ted's liking than Lyndon Johnson had been—perhaps in part for the same reason: He was invading territory that in Ted's mind had been staked out for the Kennedys.

— 4 —

THE Kennedy clan has always conceived of itself as a close little band against the world. When besieged by adversity they gather more tightly together and look to their ammunition. This happened when Bob was killed, again after Chappaquiddick, again in the early seventies when George McGovern and his brand of liberalism—Ted's own brand as well—were given a bad drubbing in the election. It happened finally with the swing of the national climate toward conservatism in the later 1970's.

More than any other single factor the we-against-the-world motif operated to firm up Ted's allegiance to revealed liberal doctrine. After 1968, when he stood alone as the last survivor, the "we" went beyond the Kennedys to his band of friends, aides, and academic advisers who, along with his brothers' children and his own, came to make up the new Kennedy entourage.

But the long years under the men he so disliked meant that —both with Bobby and alone—Ted had the sense of being in effect a government-in-exile, awaiting a happier time when it could return to power. Among many voters too the suspenseful waiting for the ascension of the legitimate heirs formed an essential part of the Kennedy mystique.

One has to add that Chappaquiddick also played a part in Ted's increasingly explicit liberalism. The first somewhat favorable response to Ted's TV speech was followed by a wave of hostility, with the dominant criticism Ted's failure both of courage and compassion. This was deeply wounding to Ted's self-image, especially since courage had been the core of the family code, and compassion had been the political signature of his welfare-state liberalism.

Almost inevitably there was a new urgency in identifying with a liberal stand that would exclude both the craven and the hard of heart. Ted's best way of showing the nation and himself that his compassion had not failed was to hold fast to his championship of federal programs for the young, poor, distressed, and helpless. His best way of showing that his courage had not faltered, at a time of a heavy undertow toward conservatism, in the latter 1970's, was to keep his course arrow-straight for the shores of the liberal secular City of Man.

The body of a public man's positions is a composite of everything he has thought, felt, and experienced, projected for public view as an outward image of what he is like inwardly. At that point the public image becomes itself an artifact, employed to do most good and least damage to his political career. This mix of the inward, the expressive, and the tactical is true of every politician, deliberately or intuitively. But in Ted's case—given the turbulence of his private and public life—the effort to make his public positions fit the needs of his image and self-image became even more pressing.

Take two cases that raised the question of expediency and principle. Both came in the 1970's, when there were treacherous crosscurrents of conservatism and liberalism. On July 4, 1973 Ted paid a visit to Governor George Wallace, at Decatur, Alabama. It took the nation, and probably Wallace, by surprise: In temperament as well as historical position they were a universe apart. In an interview I had with Wallace some weeks later he was clearly delighted at the crow-eating visit, which he interpreted as a cynical move by Ted to give himself a new conservative image. That was also how most liberals viewed it. I saw it, at the time, as an early bit of evidence that Ted was testing the political weather for a possible presidential try in 1976.

The move was wasted. The busing issue was an agonizing one for Ted, as for many legislators. It had been Bob's strategy, in his New Politics, to appeal for equality of access for blacks without cutting himself off from his links with the white ethnics, including Irish, Italian, and Slavic Catholics. Ted did his best to follow that lead, walking a delicate line between the demands of the blacks and the fears of the white ethnics. In fact, several of his early votes had been against busing.

In the wake of a federal judge's ruling to enforce desegregation in the Boston schools a strong, emotional anti-busing movement developed. Rashly or courageously, Ted tried to play a conciliator role and made an appeal at an anti-busing rally in his Boston home ground. He was received with a stony hostility that turned to threats and violence. He staged a prudent retreat with the help of the police. This wounding experience, at the hands of "my own people," firmed up his final acceptance of the traditional liberal position on busing. There were no more symbolic visits to the Wallaces of the American Heartland.

Despite these lacerating encounters, which came rarely, Ted's enjoyment of the Senate experience has been genuine and deep. Every public figure can recall some phase of his life that has been glowing for him, his remembered golden age. For Ted it has been the Senate years, which span his early manhood from thirty-one to a still buoyant forty-eight. He likes the job, the setting, the maneuvering, the tussling with substantive issues, the trade-offs, even the chores. If there is a tutelary deity in Ted's life, like a Socratic daimon, it attends him in his Senate post.

— 6 —

MIDWAY between Bob's death and Chappaquiddick, in late December 1968, there was an episode that illustrates how much weight Ted placed on the judgment of his colleagues, on being "a Senate man." For reasons still obscure, even to his closest aides, he decided to make a bid for Senator Russell Long's post as Assistant Majority Leader, or Democratic Whip.

Was it, now that he stood alone, to test and prove himself as the surviving Kennedy, able to pull a surprising coup at will? Was it—after refusing the draft bid at the Democratic Convention in July—a way of demonstrating his strength and prestige, and saying he would have to be reckoned with next time? Was it his own form of self-actualization: an effort to define himself apart from his dead brothers? Or was it another instance of an erratic decision by an impulse-dominated man in a time of great personal suffering?

I doubt whether Ted himself could explain his mixture of motives. It was a strange thing to do, at that time, for this man. My own guess is that he did it *because* it was strange, a move entirely his own, not something that Jack or Bob would have done. It was the drive that dominated him during that twilight period of violence and grief—to show himself as his own kind of man, not a rubber-stamp copy of someone else.

The surprise element was the disproportion of it. Here was a man who could probably have had the presidential nomination only a few months earlier, in July. Now, having turned down a campaign for the Presidency, here he was, making a bid for a secondary tactical party post in the Senate.

It made little objective tactical sense. But psychologically it might have been his way of saying that, as a young man still, he was for the moment content with being a captain in the Senate planning group, not Commander in Chief of the nation—that he was ready to earn his way, do hard, unglamorous work, and tie himself down with Senate chores. It was a strange way for a President-in-the-making to behave, but it was *his* strange way.

Once Ted had decided to run he did the politicking well, made scores of phone calls, touched all the bases. The party moguls, South and North, who could have blocked him chose not to. It was so little to ask, by a man who could have had so much. He still had to sweat for it, but in effect they opened the gates of the club for him to drive in.

Poor Russell Long, caught off his guard, could marshal only a ragged defense of his post. He was a drinker, something of a blowhard, and had lost prestige with the Senate. Ted won the vote handsomely, faced the cameras, promised a more activist role in the post. At the moment it was a triumph for him. He knew he had magic with Democratic voters nationally. What he valued just as much was his acceptance by his Senate colleagues. It was a technical post, not media-oriented, with tasks to be pursued almost covertly, by intricate maneuvers in the corridors of power. But it was a glowing moment of triumph for him.

— 7 —

SOME six months later, before he had really had time to prove himself, he was in disgrace because of Chappaquiddick. So much that he had tried patiently to build was undone. The Majority Leader, Mike Mansfield, welcomed him back, and other Senate notables came over to clasp his hand, embrace him. It was moving, but Kennedy was now a walking wounded case, vulnerable from every side. The assault in time came from Senator Robert Byrd of West Virginia, who had functioned as a go-fer for Democrats in the post of Secretary to the Democratic Conference.

But it didn't come for another sixteen months. During that stretch Ted worked hard on his own legislative priorities, as well as the Whip job. He was especially active in the eighteen-year-old voting franchise, which he proposed to attach as a rider to the voting rights extension bill. He was also deeply involved with the elaborate, successful effort to defeat Nixon's nomination of Judge

B. Harold Carswell to the Supreme Court, an effort largely sparked and guided by members of Kennedy's staff.

It was a spirited and demanding stretch for Ted. He badly needed the activity, to diminish if not blot out the memory of Chappaquiddick in his own mind, as well as the public's. In 1970 he broke into his Whip duties to campaign again in Massachusetts for the Senate—his third Senate campaign. He put in eighteen-hour days, pushing himself physically and nervously, at high tension. He won against a weak Republican opponent with 58 percent of the vote, a comedown since the last time, but lucky to win at all.

When it was over he returned to the rump session of the Senate. With the new session the long-expected challenge from "Bobby" Byrd came at last, in late January, 1971. Ted did his usual follow-up phoning, starting a month early, and was confident that he had the twenty-eight votes needed to turn back Byrd, with a few to spare. He didn't. Majority Leader Mansfield was more neutral than Ted had hoped for—a signal to Democrats that they were free to make their own choice. Byrd had worked hard as an all-purpose errand boy for many Senators, and had chits to cash in. But mostly Ted lost some key votes because of Chappaquiddick, and by his too abrasive effort to sharpen his political positions afterward. The vote was 31 to 24 against him. Several conjectural lists of the four Senate defectors were published. But it makes little difference who they were: The important fact was the fact of a Kennedy defeat.

The Whip episode had come full circle. Byrd beat Ted after Chappaquiddick much as Ted had beaten Long before Chappaquiddick. The original decision to run represented poor judgment. It opened a door to the wrong room, and when it closed again two years later it was on a chastened Kennedy who had been through a season of hell. He came out of it, without the Whip job, once again a freewheeling Senator, feeling secure in his Senate berth, as philosophic as he could be in his lacerated state, to face the rest of the seventies and move on into the eighties.

2

Intimacy Relations

— 1 —

THE IMAGE of Edward Kennedy as the "good Senator" in public life is often contrasted with the image of the "swinger" and "playboy" in private life. It is distorting to stress either aspect of his life to the neglect of the other. It is also distorting, in writing of his less-than-private life, to confine ourselves to the episodes that have evoked so much publicity.

We will not get a whole view of Ted if we deal only with the public man, and with Thanatos, the death principle that so conspicuously haunted his public and personal life together. For there is always also the Eros principle, which is the principle not only of sexuality and love, but the life principle with all its affirmations. With Ted, Eros was lived out in all his intimacy relations, throughout the spectrum of his life, with parents and brothers and sisters, wife and children, the families of Jack and Bob, the extramarital adventures and relationships, the close friendships.

In the case of a political figure there are complex bonds of relation that Eros has with power, and both are affected by the intense *publicness* that goes with power, for good and ill.

I have described earlier the family constellation within which Ted grew up, but I turn now to his whole developmental story as expressed in his intimacy relations within that frame. There was a benign conspiracy between his father and mother to bring up the

145

children—and especially the boys—in a planful and controlling way. That was the prime shared purpose that made them cohesive and enduring as a pair-bond.

Joe Kennedy, as father, was always the prime influence. But with the years, with Joe's absences in the first phase and his political interests in the second, there was a shifting of oversight, with Rose increasingly taking over. Joe played a far greater role in the development of Joe Jr. and Jack, Rose in the development of Bob and Ted, as well as the girls. As the lateborn son, Ted's relation to his mother thus assumes a greater weight for his development, as important as the father-son relation.

No one who studies the Kennedy family material can have any doubt about Rose's strength and about her impact on her sons and daughters. She was a controlled and controlling woman, who took charge of the most minute details in her children's lives, while she left the larger outlines to her husband. In many ways it was the details, year after year, that counted in their character formation. She saw first of all to their religious devotion, an area in which Bob and Ted were more responsive than the older boys. In fact, she felt at one point that Ted might be a priest—a choice of vocation frequently held by younger sons in the families of Irish countrymen.

She drilled her children incessantly, in table manners, deportment, dress, newspaper quizzes, information games. No drill sergeant in a military academy was ever more obsessively concerned with gun and dress drill than Rose was with the orderly preparation of her sons for their life opportunities. Ted, as the youngest, was the low boy on the totem pole in these games, and his mother sometimes primed him with the answers so that he could shine in the competition with the others.

A dedication of a recent book of his writings signed by Ted, addressed to his mother, recalls her with an amused affection:

> She could diagram a sentence, bisect an angle in geometry, or conjugate a Latin verb. She could spot a hole in a sock from a hundred yards away. She could catch an error in our grammar,

or sense a wandering eye at the grace before our meals. She could recite "The Midnight Ride of Paul Revere," name the capital of any nation in the world, and bring alive the history of every place we went.

Her concern with her sons was that they should be the right material for her experiment in mothering great men. "I had made up my mind," she said, "to raise my children as perfectly as possible. What greater aspiration and challenge can there be for a mother than the hope of raising a great son or daughter?" The operative words are "perfectly" and "great." Like her husband, Rose was a perfectionist. When their sons failed to come in first in any competition—whether in school or sports or whatever—the parents wanted to know why. Their approbation always depended on high achievement. The children may well have perceived it as a *quid pro quo* equation in which love was bartered for success in competitions.

Note also that as a mother Rose wanted to raise "great" children—not just tender or sensitive, capable of relating and loving and receiving love, not a many-sided whole person but a "great" man or a "great" woman.

One of them did indeed become great and another was reaching for greatness, when both were cut down. As for Ted, he has long been the son of whom greatness has been expected—waiting in the wings, as it were, to come through like a Kennedy, but not quite certain that he can deliver the lines.

From his father he got not a model of greatness itself but at least some intimation of it, in setting the pace of his life, dreaming the dreams, suggesting a style of macho behavior in relations with women. From his mother he got an ideal of impossible tenderness, strength, and perfection that he could never hope to recapture in a wife or in any other woman. From both his parents he got a demand for greatness in their sons, and a pattern of acceptance and love conditioned upon his winning in the game of life.

To do justice to the patriarch we must add that he came to modify what he had said to them about always needing to succeed.

As they grew up and met with reverses he tried to hearten them with a philosophy of the success of failure. "It's the best thing that ever happened to you," he would tell one son or another, pointing out that he needed the reverse in order to try harder. But the fact was, of course, that he remained success-oriented, cheering the boys on to see in defeat the good that would lead to success.

Rose, it must be added, outwardly accepted Ted's mishaps with the same fortitude she showed in accepting the more anguishing tragedies in the family. Her combination of piety and stoicism armored her against the deaths, as it appeared to armor her against the shock of Chappaquiddick. After Ted's return to Hyannisport, after that ghastly night and the ghastly day that followed it, when the news broke on all the wires and the reporters besieged the family compound, it was Rose who remained calm and even cheerful amid the general gloom, giving Ted her unqualified support. But whatever explicit support his mother gave him now could not undo the years of conditioning for achievement and success nor erase the grim feeling, after Chappaquiddick, that he had indeed failed her. In Gregory Bateson's terms there was a built-in double message in family communication between parents and children, and Ted had to react to the contradictions it contained.

— 2 —

IT is not surprising that Ted, even more than his brothers, should have had difficulties in relating to women. Much has been written in recent years on Jack's erotic life, less on Bob's. Like Joe Jr. before him, Jack was popular with young women, both seeker and sought-after. Rose noted in her letters that he was swamped with invitations to parties and dances, and relished them. Before the war Joe Jr. poached at times on Jack's territory, pushing the rueful younger brother aside and appropriating some morsel for himself.

In the competitive spirit of the family, handed down from father to sons, each new woman was an added conquest as well as an article of adornment—new evidence of having won in a family-sanctioned contest.

For the younger brothers—Bob seven or eight years after Jack, Ted a similar distance from Bob—the ever-present vivid example of father and brothers was always there. We can only guess how much of Bob's inner turbulence in adolescence came from the conflicting drives of sexuality and the macho models of his father and brothers with the repressive religious standards he had learned. There was something about Bob's sense of virtue in the early days that made him a Malvolio figure of censoriousness for the older boys: "Dost thou think, because thou art virtuous, there shall be no more cakes and ale?" Yet Bob was mostly to overcome it, and had not only a happy and fruitful marriage but at least one extramarital affair, publicized after his death.

Jack's affairs were legion. An early one, which surfaced later, was an affair he carried on while stationed in San Francisco during the war with a mysterious beauty who was under the surveillance of Navy Intelligence. When it had gone too far for security the Navy spirited the lady away and sent Jack off on PT-boat assignment, where he was shot up, became a war hero, and got his start on a political career.

There were many others, both before and after his marriage to Jacqueline Bouvier, who, along with her beauty and intelligence, had enough spirit and strength to last out a marriage compounded of love and hostility. If all the stories about his women are to be believed, Jack Kennedy as President turned the White House into a Deer Park, like the Sun King at Versailles. There was also an affair with a woman who was the mistress of a Mafia figure used by the CIA in an operation aimed at killing Fidel Castro. Jack constantly walked a danger line in his liaisons, as he did in his foreign policy encounters with Khrushchev and Castro. He was like Nietzsche's rope-dancer. In the end the danger line became a death line.

— 3 —

LIKE Jack, Ted was drawn to danger, but more in his private than his public life. He had Jack's attitude toward women: to triumph as often as possible, but to keep from yielding his heart and commitment. They both had difficulty in relating with any emotional depth to a woman, or seeing her as other than a sex object and a field for conquest.

Their difference was one of style. From the time he was in Congress and especially after his marriage, in the Senate and Presidency, Jack's affairs were known only to a small group of friends, including some in the press. He used prudence and a sense of what was fitting behavior for his position, and concern for his wife's feelings. It was not until his death that most of the stories broke.

Ted's affairs have been more public. The description of the life-style of the test pilots in Tom Wolfe's *The Right Stuff* fits Ted's style: "hard drinking, hard driving and the private pursuit of manliness." For Ted too this had an exhilarating reality beyond the everyday dullness and hypocrisy. After some hard driving to get to a party he was not averse to some very public hard drinking and an unprivate pursuit of a pretty girl he has danced with, and found amenable.

The English anthropologist, Mary Douglas, has suggested that the symbolic world of a variety of societies polarized around *purity* and *danger.* Can we venture that the Kennedy brothers felt themselves drawn, like their father, to the archetypal figure of the forbidden temptress, the Astarte who is dangerous and seductive, and were held back by another archetypal vision of perfect purity —their mother—so perfect as to be unattainable?

Given a mother who offered only a conditional love Ted tried to find a wife who would have his mother's beauty and purity, but also love him unconditionally. Joan seemed such a figure—a lovely, long-haired blonde, a student at Manhattanville, the Catholic college of his mother and his sister Jean—who had done some modeling and some social work, would raise a large family as his mother had done, and would grace his coming political career, wherever it might go.

— 4 —

THE story of Ted and Joan's marriage, which should with luck have remained private, became inevitably a staple of the women's magazines and the Sunday features. It is the classic story of two attractive, wealthy young people of good family who seem to have everything, but who misjudge each other and themselves and their needs.

It is hard to say when the marriage started to go wrong, but the ingredients for disaster were there. Joan was a vulnerable girl and needed a protective husband to nourish her fragile self-esteem. She found instead an immature young man who had always been protected by his father in a home controlled by his mother, who needed support himself and faced crises badly. When, like his father, he turned elsewhere for consolation he expected his wife to be as understanding as his mother had been. But Joan was not Rose, or Jackie or Ethel Kennedy, as she would have liked to be, all rolled in one. She idolized the Kennedys and was frightened by them. She had a weak self-image,. and instead of being stoic about Ted's wanderings, she was dismayed, and the hurt went deep.

At one point she appeared at political functions at Washington in bizarre, conspicuous outfits, like a wife hoping to attract her husband's (and the world's) attention but also managing to hurt him. She found coping with the children difficult. The Chappaquiddick incident, coming in the midst of their strained period, may also in part have sprung from it and deepened the crisis. If Mary Jo Kopechne was the primary victim of the accident, Joan Kennedy was the second one. She had a miscarriage soon after. Not surprisingly she developed a drinking problem.

She is a sensitive woman who hates the way the media have

intruded into her marriage, and shrinks from the headlines Ted gets. She moved to Boston, entered a graduate program in teaching, went into therapy, built her own circle of friends, and has managed to achieve a new life and a new self-confidence. When Ted decided in 1979 on his run for the Presidency she approved of it, campaigned with him, openly discussed her "problem," and touchingly supported his candidacy.

Ted has proved a better father to his three children, Ted Jr., Kara, and Patrick, than a husband. Patrick suffers from a severe allergy problem. Ted Jr. developed a bone cancer that made a leg amputation imperative. Ted took charge, maturely and responsibly, while Joan was away. He is a good father, tender and imaginative. He has also been surrogate father, as the surviving Kennedy male, to his brothers' children, including Bob's and Ethel's large brood. When their children have been in trouble Ted has cut into his Senate duties to be wherever he is needed, and stand in their father's place. It is a very real way of picking up the fallen standard, a human and important one.

This too is Eros—this life-affirming role as father and surrogate father, along with his continuing relation to his mother and sisters and brothers-in-law. At forty-eight Ted is scarcely a patriarch, yet with the succession of deaths he has taken over his father's role as head of the clan. It is as if, with the father's death, his *mana* had been passed to Ted. There was a strong progenitive strain in Joe Sr., as in Bob. It shows up also in Ted, not in siring many children but in a nurturing concern for them. If responsibilities can make a man responsible, there are more than enough of them here to do the trick.

— 6 —

NOR can we omit another phase of Eros—the relation of a politician and political orator to the people, and theirs to him. This is a shared trait of the Kennedy brothers, who have had a physical vitality and electric presence to which the voters responded. It is true of Ted, as it was of his brothers. His entrance into a room or hall evokes fire.

There is the joy and agony of campaigning—the dog-tiredness of it, the living through the rejections, but also the reaching to another level of energy, which the long-distance runner and the true campaigner know. There is more to it than obeying the ancestral voice that tells Ted to do his damndest in every speech, press conference, campaign rally. It is also the dramatic rapport at a high moment between leader and people, speaker and audience. The exchange on issues is indispensable, but the exchange of recognition goes deeper.

There are photos of Ted in a crowd, reaching his hands out to as many as he can grasp, while scores are reaching their hands out to him. "I touched him," a woman cries, or a child. "He shook my hand," an old man recalls much later. It is condescending to write these off as vanity or hysteria. The touch of the charismatic leader, like the king's touch, retains magic. It is the recognition incarnate, as much part of the Eros principle as the interlocking of selves in sexuality.

I doubt strongly whether Ted's intimacy relations, and his breaking of the accepted sexual codes, are what bar his way to the Presidency. They turn many off, yes. But they are also an integral part of the Kennedy legend, which turns more people on. No exploration of the legend can ignore the role that the maleness of the Kennedy males played in its shaping.

What is much more at issue with any political leader is his wholeness and clarity as a person, which affect his judgment and his ability to make and carry out decisions. It is here that his pattern of intimacy relations becomes important. He learned young and permanently that love carries danger. The caution at the core may be the reciprocal of his warmth and ease in public, and his nurturing affection for the young. If Ted has shown himself flawed in his relations with women the flaw is not in his strong sexual drive but in the problems he has with loving and accepting love—with true intimacy in a sustained way.

3

Why Ted Slept: 1968, 1972, 1976

— 1 —

Soon after Bob was killed, Allard Lowenstein encountered Ted in the elevator at the Hospital of the Good Samaritan, in Los Angeles, taking his brother's sheet-covered body down to the autopsy room. Lowenstein emotionally implored Ted to "take the leadership." "Now that Bobby's gone, you're all we've got." Ted responded—by Lowenstein's account—"with great politeness" and said "he would carry on."

Lowenstein was probably right. Ted Kennedy's best chance to become President was in 1968 when he least expected it and was least likely to make a clear judgment about it. The real point to the whole 1968 campaign episode is the light it sheds on how Ted's mind and will operated in the first great decision of his political career on his own, and on his evolving attitude to the Presidential nomination over the years.

It started with rumblings of support for Ted as President, only a month after Bob's killing. They seemed spontaneous. A Harris poll showed that Ted's name on the ticket in either spot would add five million votes to the Democratic ticket. "Draft Ted" movements sprang up. The liberal support for Gene McCarthy was crumbling, and McCarthy himself seemed apathetic. The Democratic nomination was up for grabs. The backing for Hubert Humphrey, the "power brokers" who ran the big city machine, was cardboard stuff, and the Peace Now group was bent on destroying him. Richard Daley, the doughty mayor of Chicago, was a symbol of the change taking place. Where he had been cool to Bob as candidate he was active in pursuit of Ted, and it was pretty clear that others like him would follow.

Ted found it too much to handle. "What is it all about?" he asked friends. He was puzzled and confused. Bob had to sweat for every primary he won, yet here, with the convention a week away, were the Democratic President-makers offering him the nomination. Ted was wary; the loyalties of the city bosses were thin and transitory. When Daley, tracking him down on a boat at Hyannisport, urged him to come to the convention, Ted sent Steve Smith instead to make soundings.

The Standard Club, where Smith established himself, became the smoke-filled room on which convention leaders converged, carrying assurances for Ted. Several of Ted's aides set up phone banks from the Kennedy family's merchandise mart to the convention floor, and began tallying delegates. When Ted still held back Daley remarked to Smith, "Jack Kennedy knew how to count and Robert Kennedy knew how to count, and your young man had better learn quick."

Daley had to get an answer fast, Yes or No. He was under strong pressure from Lyndon Johnson to support Hubert Humphrey, whom LBJ only disliked while he loathed every Kennedy on principle, although Ted less as a person. Daley was no idealist. Bob had rubbed him the wrong way but Bob was dead and everything was changing. The anti-war cohorts and the hippies were flooding into Chicago by the thousands, pitching their tents in the parks, taunting the police, chanting "Dump the Hump." Daley saw Ted as the only way to keep from losing the election with Humphrey. The other decision-makers—Mike DiSalle of Ohio, John Bailey of Connecticut, Jess Unruh of California—had similar stakes. They might not have gone for Bob, but they had everything to gain with Ted, and above all they didn't want Richard Nixon.

If Ted couldn't count the counting was done for him. One

tally of sure delegate votes came to 1200, another (including that of Steve Smith) was 1400. The vote needed to win was 1312. Smith, himself conservative and skeptical about the whole venture, later said that Ted "could have had it, without question." The turning point seemed to come when Gene McCarthy, in a ten-minute conversation with Smith, was outwardly encouraging but shied away from making the nominating speech for Ted. Sick about Ted's seesawing, Daley gave up. Smith flew back East, and Ted called Humphrey to assure him of his support.

The curious, intricate, baffling 1968 episode was closed. Humphrey was nominated amidst the bloody clash of Daley's police with the demonstrators, LBJ was halfhearted in his support of Humphrey, the peace liberals committed mayhem on him, and Richard Nixon, delighted with Ted's withdrawal, moved into the power citadel he had longed for.

How explain Ted's behavior? Ted said later that he owed it to the memory of Bob's "concerns" to "explore" the overtures on the Presidency. He may also have hoped to move the convention closer to a liberal peace position. But, he said, he had never seriously thought of making the run, and had never had the intent to "encourage it or pursue it."

His statements had that stuffy, stilted quality that Ted took on when he wanted to sound like a statesman. They contrast with his speech at Worcester, Massachusetts, only three days before Smith left for Chicago, which was gung ho for action. There was "no place to hide," he said in presenting a new position on the war strikingly close to that of the peace group. He was ready to pick up the fallen standard of his brothers.

This could, of course, have meant only that he would not be deterred from an active Senatorship and a peace campaign by the tragedies in his family and the danger of becoming a target. It would then be consistent with refusing to run for the Presidency. But it was not consistent with the peek-a-boo tactics that Ted displayed that had him at once hiding from the Presidency and setting up phone banks to the convention floor to get reports from the state delegations.

The truth was that Ted could count, and wanted to, but didn't have the will to follow up on the count. The reasons he later gave—his youth, the dynasty question, his concern for his family, his not having the heart for campaigning so soon after the murder —were all true enough. But if they were then it made no sense to go through the elaborate charade with Daley, Bailey, DiSalle, Unruh, and McCarthy. Ted couldn't have it both ways at the time and he can't have it both ways in the judgment by historians.

I suspect that Ted suffered confusion of roles. This "was Bobby's year," Ted said, as his final explanation. He was trying to use his father's principle of hierarchial succession, and to become the patriarch. Responding to family protests about running Ted for the Senate his father had once said, "it's Ted's turn." Ted could now have said, "This was Bobby's year, but I want to try to complete it for him." Instead he used the phrase retrospectively, to inhibit his own action, not, as his father had done, prospectively, to release himself.

Judging from Steve Smith's later account, Ted and he felt that, however probable the nomination, Ted couldn't win the election. But this was a dubious political prediction of the summer and fall mood of 1968. Better than anyone else—better certainly than Hubert Humphrey—Ted could have welded together the diverse elements of the "Great Coalition" that had come apart with the war, and could have denied millions of votes to Nixon that came to him in reaction to the Chicago violence. In fact, with Ted as candidate, and the support of the peace group at the convention, the confrontation might have been averted, Ted would have been in the White House instead of Nixon, and both Chappaquiddick and Watergate would never have occurred. We can never know for certain how it would have come out. I suspect that Ted muffed his chance through a failure of nerve. "I just didn't have the stomach for that," Ted has said. "I didn't feel I was personally qualified for the run." This comes closest of all his statements, then and later, to the truth.

It would have been even closer if he had said, not "for the run" but "for the job." The job that his father and brothers had talked of for years, which had shone like a glittering city for conquest, which Jack won until he was wasted and Bobby never reached, which, looking back after their deaths, seemed more beckoning and formidable than ever—this job, the Presidency of the United States: Was he really up to it?

. It was a question that Jack and Bob had never put to themselves, because they knew it couldn't be answered except by trying it out. Ted's advisers were mostly against it, for all the reasons Ted felt, including the risk that it would be viewed as a characteristic Kennedy arrogance for Ted to run when his brother's body was scarcely cold. But Ted was not a gambler, nor even daring in seizing the chance that was there. The Presidency, he was to find, is not for those who want to have it served on a platter, like some delicacy they can taste and nibble at.

—— 2 ——

TED'S decision against running for the Presidency in 1972 came out of a context very different from that of 1968. In the earlier campaign he had to make his decision during the confusions of the terrible summer of 1968.

The four years between 1968 and 1972 had been years of lacerating testing. Now at forty, there was some sense of respite. He had emerged from Chappaquiddick a survivor, saved his Senate seat and, despite his loss of the second Whip fight, he was a member of the select Senate club. Would he now, in 1972, stick by his public promise to stay with his Senate loyalty, forsaking all others, including the presidential temptation?

Ted said in the fall of 1969 that he would keep his Senate seat and not run for President. But his presidential intentions were again the chief media and conversation piece of the 1972 precampaign. Politicians are known to be strange creatures who make promises easily and can as easily retreat from them. The press and public regard it indulgently as game-playing. They hold politicians up to stricter standards of sexual morality and financial honesty than others, but settle for looser standards of political promise-keeping. If Ted, after all, were to run for President in 1972 there would have been only a minor flurry, not a major storm, over his change of heart, especially if a draft movement had developed.

Again the guessing game began, and again Ted entered the game he has repeatedly played with the public—the teasing role he loves best in politics. Through the late winter and spring of 1972 he crisscrossed the country, from Charleston to Portland and from San Diego to West Virginia, crowding engagements into every month. He talked to Jaycees, hospital workers, minority groups, labor leaders, doctors. He spoke to the Washington Press Club and the ADA Convention, and held his health subcommittee hearings across the map. Yet all the time he said, publicly and privately, that he was not running. If he wasn't a candidate he was putting on a mystifying show.

The reasons against running, as he recounted them in December 1971 to Jack's biographer, James MacGregor Burns—later to be Ted's biographer as well—were mostly his family responsibilities and again his own need for a respite from tension. They should not have been decisive if he cared deeply about what he called the "disarray" of the country. He told Burns that we needed to put the violent sixties behind us a bit more, and another interviewer that "it feels wrong in my gut."

A "gut" feeling is the distillation, deep within, of all the crosscurrents of mind, judgment, and psyche. Despite the lapse of four anguished years Ted in 1972 was, in terms of striking a trial balance for a decision, still the same man he was in 1968. He still found the Senate to be a clean, well-lit place and the road to the Presidency stormy and unpredictable. He still had doubts about his adequacy to make the voyage. Once more he played out this inner debate within the frame of a teasing no-candidate candidacy. It gave him a chance to be in the thick of the mock battle as a *presidential politician,* even while he avoided the actual dangers of being a declared candidate.

He seemed to put that real battle in a secondary place. Speaking of the nomination he said to Burns that "Maybe some candidate will take hold and run off with it," which would be "fine" with him. George McGovern did exactly that, and ran on a record and platform almost identical with Ted's, and was trounced by Richard Nixon, carrying only Massachusetts. Ted had sensed in his "gut," I suspect, that Nixon was far stronger in 1972 than in 1968, and left it to McGovern to be the victim. But in that case why the whole preliminary display of campaign muscle, except as an elaborate mummery?

Was it to send a message that he was politically alive and well in 1972 and would be around in 1976?

— 3 —

IF Ted's 1972 tactics were a waiting operation for 1976 they seemed to be paying off when that campaign year arrived. Ted's own brand of liberalism—little different in substance from McGovern's—seemed to survive by the personal cachet he gave it. The McGovern debacle left no one to assume leadership of the liberal Democrats, and Ted supplied the need. He had a reelection contest for the Senate to face, but it offered no problems. He was riding high, and there was no one of note to challenge him for the presidential nomination in 1976 if he were determined to get it.

The one question mark was the possible effect of Watergate on Ted by its impact on Chappaquiddick. It was a potential battle of symbolic scandals, with Chappaquiddick less political but on another level more tragic.

The relation—or non-relation—of Ted and Nixon deserves more study than it has had. Nixon hated Ted and Ted despised Nixon. Ted fought Nixon for years, on *issues,* but passed up two chances to face him directly in presidential combat in 1968 and 1972—as his brother Jack had once done in 1960. Did he fear that he might fail the test of battle that his brother had won? When he said that he "had no stomach" for it in 1968, and that "It was Bobby's year," was he also saying that it let him, Ted, off the hook, and that he couldn't match Bob's moral ferocity against Nixon? When he passed up the chance again in 1972 it suggested that the state of Ted's stomach had not improved.

Nixon could only have been joyful in 1968 that the one man he feared most, after the death of Jack and Bob Kennedy, had bowed out. But he remained savage about Ted. Right after Chappaquiddick the palace guard sent the ineffable Tony Ulasewicz to Hyannisport, to pose as a reporter, ask needling questions, look into the phone calls on the night of the death. H. R. Haldeman wanted to have the FBI set a continuous watch on Ted in the hope of trapping him in some exploitable situation, but settled for a spot check. When Ted removed himself as candidate again in 1972, he removed the only Democrat with a good chance to win, even though Nixon, off on a counter-counterculture values binge, would have used Chappaquiddick ruthlessly.

The Kennedy Senate staff was on the scent of Watergate as early as September 1972. But Ted, even in his Judiciary Committee role, was symbolically the wrong Senator to go after Watergate, and Mike Mansfield wisely chose Senator Sam Ervin instead. The irony of Watergate for Ted was that while it summed up everything he had against Nixon, Ted was immobilized by his own behavior at Chappaquiddick and his failure to clarify it. It was galling to have to remain silent because—as Barry Goldwater put it quite nakedly—there could be no "moralizing" and stone-throwing by anyone who himself lived in a glass house. This particular glass house cast a long shadow.

Curiously this was not how the people themselves felt. The polls in the spring of 1974 showed Kennedy leading Gerald Ford by 50 to 39. In July, the fifth anniversary of Chappaquiddick, the reappraisals—expecially one by Robert Sherrill in *The New York Times*—were severe in their judgment. It was a hard time also for Joan and the children. Ted was beset with his personal problems at the moment when the Democratic chances for a 1976 victory seemed brightest. The Nixon regime had collapsed and the Vietnam peace, purchased at the price of so much blood, had fallen apart. This was Ted's best opportunity since 1968. Would he finally seize it?

The manner of making his decision was striking. There was no general input, no gathering of the clan, no thrashing out of debits and credits. There was only, in August 1974, a stroll on the beach for an hour or two by Kennedy and his trusted aide, Dave Burke, who had been against Ted running in 1968 and was against it now. Both men strove to canvass the pros and cons with as much detachment as they could muster. Out of it came Ted's "Great Renunciation."

It was a Shermanlike decision—"firm, final and unconditional"—not to accept a nomination or draft. Chappaquiddick, he said, was not a factor ("I can live with my testimony."), nor was his own safety a "major" factor. It was his family "responsibilities"—meaning primarily Ted Jr.'s amputation and his fear of his father's death, and Joan's alcoholism and her anguish about their marriage.

It was an understandable decision, but it leaves a gaping question. Even within Ted's own frame of expressed motives, why did he have to rule himself out two years in advance of the nominating convention? His declared reason was that he wanted to give other candidates a chance to build and show their strength. It was a generous gesture, even a quixotic one, but was it a wise move for a man who ultimately wanted to be President?

Ted was asked whether he would run in 1980, and gave the expected answer that the Democrats would win and the new President would be running for a second term. He turned out to be right; his renunciation was exactly what an obscure Georgia Governor called Jimmy Carter was hoping for. He had started earlier but with Ted out of the running he broke away from the field of amiable nonentities and made it. If Ted still had a hope of running for the Presidency in 1980 he was either dooming his party, if it lost, to four years of powerlessness until then, or else —as it turned out—he created his own executioner.

Even the more credible ground for renouncing the race was questionable. Joan had been fragile earlier and continued to be: Ted's renunciation didn't save her or their marriage. His closeness to his children was not affected one way or the other: Actually, when they later accompanied him on his 1980 campaign and got a taste of the action, they came closer to him.

Ted must also have known that his statement would not end this third quadrennial effort to draft him. No matter how hard he tried to quash the boomlets they kept cropping up. During 1975 the pressure for Ted to run increased. His friend, Rep. "Tip" O'Neill, of Massachusetts, set off a minor flurry by reporting that Ted really wanted the nomination and had asked him to "keep me alive." It must have been half-playful, half-plaintive. For many he was the political star symbol they hungered for.

Nor could he in regal fashion pass on the Kennedy legacy to his brother-in-law, Sargent Shriver, who had run with George McGovern on his hapless 1972 ticket and who declared for the Presidency in September 1975. By making his move two years early Ted cut himself off from having any influence on the nomination. Both Shriver and Morris Udall, the candidate closest to Ted's brand of liberalism, were knocked out early. The man who emerged to don the crown that Ted had thrice refused, Jimmy Carter, was a small-town Georgian, of no particular family or style and no Washington experience, a self-created man, with an evangelical fervor that promised a personal pipeline to God—yet also a man who ploughed on to his Presidential purpose.

"Deep down," a reporter asked Ted, "do you want to be President?" Ted's answer was Yes. But the question remains open. Every time he was asked such a question his answer has run in terms of carrying on the purposes of his brothers. It was not the answer of his brother Jack—to use it as a summit place to stand, so he could move the world. Nor was it the answer of the driven Presidents—a Johnson, Nixon, Carter—to reach the Presidency because it was *there,* a supreme challenge to their capacity to beat others and transcend themselves.

One must ask whether Ted wanted the Presidency mainly

because it was expected of him. He was happy in his Senate harbor: Why should he venture into the dangerous presidential sea? Someone should have recalled to him Joseph Conrad's injunction: "Yield yourself to the destructive element, and it will bear you up."

Three times he had the chance and each time he found a different set of reasons for refusing. Each time, as it turned out, he was wrong, in varying degrees. His first chance came in 1968, before the Chappaquiddick curse descended on him, and while the torment and guilt about Bob's death still lay on the country. The second time was chancier, in 1972, three years after Chappaquiddick, with Nixon more formidable than in 1968. The third chance, in 1976—post-Watergate, post-Vietnam, with the Republicans badly split between Gerald Ford and Ronald Reagan—was close to any politician's dream. Yet Ted walked away from it two years early, clearly mistrusting his capacity to say No when the pressures got intense.

CHAPTER VI

ACTING OUT THE LEGEND: THE CAMPAIGN OF 1979-80

1

Gage of Battle: Why Ted Ran

— 1 —

I T WASN'T long after the 1976 election that Ted Kennedy began to feel rueful at having cleared the way for Jimmy Carter's kind of President to take power. Ted and the whole Kennedy camp were appalled at what they saw as his inexperience, amateurishness, blundering.

An earlier incident during the 1976 campaign suggests that their dislike of each other had started earlier. When Ted criticized Carter for loose talk, Carter was angry. "I'm not going to kiss Kennedy's ass," he told aides.

Ted was watching Carter's slipping polls. Not even Camp David, with its historic rapproachement of Egypt and Israel, in the fall of 1978, was able to give a lift to his declining popularity. With the Iranian revolution it was clear that Carter had been overtaken by events and had neither foreseen the revolution nor been prepared for its impact on energy supplies and prices. The two interlinked events—the Iranian revolution and inflation—seemed about to dig Carter's political grave.

Every President has had at some time to run the gauntlet of bruising attacks for blunders committed or attributed. Carter had exposed himself to attacks by a tender-minded, idealistic foreign and defense policy, his mishandling of staff scandals (Bert Lance, Andrew Young), and his inability to get his programs through

Congress or to mount a credible anti-inflation campaign. As his troubles at home increased his image and credibility abroad were diminished, which in turn opened him to new troubles on both fronts. It was a deadly spiral effect.

It was also a classic case history of the role of the subjective in the growth and decline of political prestige. In his campaign Carter's fresh face, his freedom from any linkage with professional Washington politics, and his stress on love, honesty, and morality worked in his favor. Every accession of strength led to another.

But Carter came to Washington with a makeshift power base, and it seemed to crumble with the same swiftness with which it was assembled. He was largely a media product from the start, coming from thin air and seemingly about to dissolve into thin air. There is a great American blood sport of savaging the President —an almost tribal cannibalism by which the people, after having raised him to the dizzying heights of office, devour him. Having become President largely by using the image of an outsider, free of political loyalties, Carter had no loyalties to invoke when he began to blunder and needed them most. As he moved toward the nadir of his power, every failure was compounded.

— 2 —

BY the early spring of 1979 Jimmy Carter was at bay, wounded and bleeding from the shafts of his own party as well as the opposition. That was the point at which Ted Kennedy had to decide about moving in on his own party's incumbent President.

It was a fateful decision to make. In none of the three past presidential election years had he had to move so openly into opposition, not even in 1968, when Lyndon Johnson was still President—although a lame-duck President.

Yet the Johnson parallel was a seductive one for the Kennedy camp. The combined onslaught of Eugene McCarthy and Bob

Kennedy had forced Johnson into abdicating his candidacy. As long as Carter seemed a viable President, retaining support despite his weakening hold on the office, Ted kept a waiting stance. But when the attacks mounted and Carter started to crumble, Ted began to see him as a Lyndon Johnson who would succumb to a strong challenge. He might even, like LBJ, be pushed to abdicate, rather than suffer the humiliation of defeat.

If Ted had doubts about throwing down the gage of battle to an incumbent President, the dissipation of trust in Carter did much to convince him. There were few commentators who gave him much chance to salvage his earlier popular acceptance. "Dump Carter" movements proliferated.

The Carter and Kennedy camps had no illusions about each other's love. Both were watching the polls. Ted's repeated formula answer to queries about his running was, "I expect President Carter to be renominated and I expect to support him." In early May, 1979, asked how he felt about his lead in the polls, he answered, "I am heartened, but I am not going to be a candidate." On May 12 Carter was still pretending to believe that "if I ran Senator Kennedy would give me his support."

But by mid-June, Carter decided to end the pretense. At a Camp David meeting he told several congressmen, when the subject of Ted came up, "I'll whip his ass." His aides retold the story with relish. Ted took it lightly, saying the next day that he was not a candidate, "but if I were to run I would hope to win," and two days later he tried to turn it to his advantage: "I'm sure he was misquoted. What he meant to say was that he would whip inflation."

By late June, Kennedy had a 42-point lead over Carter (68–26), and by mid-August it was still a 38-point lead (63–25). By early September he was certain enough of his decision to ask for a private meeting with the President. They lunched at the White House, at first with Rosalyn Carter there, then alone.

It was then that Ted told the President he was considering a race against him. It couldn't have been a cordial conversation. Each man felt that the other was stubborn in sticking to a contest certain to divide the Democrats. Kennedy saw before him a man who had reached the nadir in leadership authority and credibility, and should—like Lyndon Johnson—renounce another term in the nation's interest. Carter saw before him a man who was there only because he was a Kennedy, who had three times failed to run when he had the chance and now picked an incumbent Democratic President to challenge.

— 3 —

THE fact was that, with his early decisive lead over Carter in the polls, Ted had moved slowly. It was a deliberate tactic in order to avoid the image of the spoiler who arrogantly plunged into the fray against his party leader. Ted said later that he had to over-come the hesitations of his mother and his wife before deciding to run. But few could accept that as the reason for the delay. More than anyone, Rose was bound to support whatever Ted decided. Joan, less so, may nevertheless have wanted to test her new control over her life circumstances and herself, and may have seen a campaign as both a phase and a sign of her new start.

Ted's real strategy of timing was to move into the contest when Carter's chances of recovery seemed slight at best, and the leadership issue was ripe to pluck. Up to that point Ted had emphasized only his Senate record of consistent liberalism. In a time of opportunist movement toward the Right by other politi-cians it was meant to show his consistency. Given the plague of criticism about Chappaquiddick it was meant to show both his courage and compassion.

It seemed amazingly to work. The media magicians who preside over the pre-election elections had Ted practically in the White House in October 1979. The Kennedy phenomenon broke all the political axioms—that a candidate must temper himself to the prevailing winds of doctrine, that he has to be a good "family man," that he can't have a wife who is a problem drinker and lives separately from him, that a man who invites gossip about his extramarital life is politically unviable, that an incumbent President operates from a stronghold impregnable to challenge within his own party, that Americans never forgive and never forget a transgressing politician, and that a major life blunder dooms a man politically forever.

Writing as a columnist during that year I must confess to my delight at this overturn of all the conventional political wisdom, and with Ted's emergence again as the leading Democratic candidate. I like unlikely stories, comebacks, reversals of the accepted and expected. Most commentators, like most of the voters polled, felt that Carter had become stuck, both in his policies and credibility, and welcomed Ted's candidacy because it widened the voters' options.

— **4** —

IT was at this point, in September 1979, that Ted shifted his strategy, making his first blunder. He talked more and more about "leadership," about Carter's absence of it and his own possession of it. If he had simply kept restating his Senate record and applied it to concrete issues of the day, he could have sustained the three themes of consistency, courage, and compassion, and might have avoided the looming pit. Instead, he couldn't resist the temptation that Carter's loss of credibility offered, and he moved brashly to set up a leadership command post in the vacuum.

Jimmy Carter and his Gerogia condottiere, who had much to learn about governing a nation but who knew how to mount a campaign, waited in ambush while Ted hammered at the leadership theme. In the last week of September 1979, they opened fire. To a group of editors Carter spoke of the "reputation" he had "for being steady in an emergency." A few days later he spoke of the danger, for a President, of "panic in a crisis." On September 25 in Queens, New York, he came closest to being explicit: "I don't think I panicked in a crisis." To be sure, he reassured Kennedy that he hadn't meant to refer to Chappaquiddick, but this was a standard politician's way of affirming what he denied, a case of naming by not naming.

Carter didn't have to do much more to draw the spectral line of attention around Ted's personal past. Perhaps he didn't even have to do that much. Those who thought that Americans were showing their capacity to forget and forgive a character lapse were reckoning without the special temper of the time.

It was a time of planetary turmoil, of a sharp anxiety about the economy, of the people's loss of self-confidence and of confidence in their leaders. It was also a time of a gut need on their part for direction and decisiveness. Ted had opened himself to attack on his crisis behavior by denying Carter's leadership qualities. Carter didn't have to appeal to Chappaquiddick: inevitably the voters were starting to raise the question in their own minds. But he made doubly sure.

Amidst the sparring it was clear that the Ted camp had reached a decision for announcing. Ted set it finally for November 7. It was almost anticlimactic since he had all along been acting as a candidate, despite his protestations. The political community was astir with anticipation. Ted's cohorts came from every direction to advise, consent, and support. A few in the group went all the way back to Jack, some thirty years, and more had advised Bob and had been with Ted in his crisis after Chappaquiddick.

In the historic, memory-drenched Faneuil Hall in Boston, on November 7, with his immediate and his extended family in attendance—including Rose and Joan Kennedy and Jacqueline Onassis—and before a standing-room-only audience of several hundred reporters, Edward M. Kennedy declared his candidacy for the Presidency of the United States. The speech he read was scarcely an inspired one. Again he hammered at the "need for leadership," and promised to be "in the thick of the action." Again he invoked the memory of both his brothers and committed himself to carrying on their work. It was a bloodless and synthetic performance, after the long buildup a curious anticlimax.

Yet it was an occasion that had never been seen in American history: a third presidential campaign by the last of three brothers. It came twenty years and four Presidencies after John Kennedy declared for the Presidency, in 1959, and eleven years after Robert Kennedy declared, in 1968. Ted had been twenty-seven on the first occasion, thirty-six on the second, and was forty-seven on the eve of his own declaration.

— 5 —

AFTER the past hesitations and refusals, why did Ted finally decide to run in the 1980 election? He faced a double problem— strategic and psychological. In strategic terms, the big argument against it was that he would have to wrest the Democratic nomination from a Democratic President, and do it with the albatross of Chappaquiddick around his neck.

On the other side was the fact of Carter's almost unparalleled drop in the polls, and the chorus of voices (including my own) that lamented a vacuum of leadership. Ted gambled that the Carter loss of support was irreversible. It was before the idea of the "volatility" of the voter, and the word itself had become encrusted, early in 1980. But unlike Lyndon Johnson, Carter was not tied into a messy, mindless war, and thus had the freedom of movement at some point to reverse the polls. Ted must have known this, but he counted on its not happening because Carter was trapped in something as deadly as the Vietnam War—a losing struggle against inflation.

It was this reasoning that led Ted to choose the economic strategy as his major road to the White House, in preference to a foreign policy strategy, where his differences with Carter were not great at the time. The economic strategy had the advantage of touching the pocketbook nerve that, in the traditional lore of politics, is held to ensure victory. Here in truth, Ted felt, was the advantage an attacker would have, that would not be undermined by events but could only be strengthened by them.

As for the albatross of Chappaquiddick, the answer to that seemed to be in the polls. The tenth anniversary of Chappaquiddick fell, as it happened, in August 1979. It brought its expected gaggle of "Chappaquiddick Revisited" articles in the Sunday sections and the magazines, including an impassioned one by John Gregory Dunne in *New West,* which took its place with Robert Sherrill's piece in *The New York Times Magazine* on the fifth anniversary. Yet the polls continued upbeat on Ted, and unwarily he and his advisers may have concluded that Ted's misdeed had been almost forgotten, if not quite forgiven.

— 6 —

AS it turned out, the polls were misleading because mostly they measured the end result in the voter attitudes and not the ingredients that led to it. Polls have only the depth of the questions put to the sample, and there were none that reached to the *mistrust potential* in the voter's mind. How much of that potential is tapped depends on the questions asked and the extent to which the mistrust issue is opened up by events.

As we shall see, that is exactly what happened. The Chappaquiddick mistrust issue wasn't strongly enough felt to make a dent in Ted's polls while they were rising or remained high. But when an event triggered it—as happened on the eve of Ted's announcement, in the Roger Mudd interview—it reinforced the newly awakened doubts and added to the downward slide of the ratings. What was not strong enough in itself to reverse Ted's high poll acceptance was strong enough, once the slide was triggered by an event, to hasten him down the slope to doom.

He could have waited out the election. One could make a case that there was every reason for him to wait. He didn't have to try for the Presidency. He had a safe Senate seat. He could wait until 1984 or 1988 or even 1992, when he would be 60, and the occasion might be less difficult. He was risking assassination, as his brothers had. He was risking failure, and if he failed he would be the first of the brothers to have it happen to him.

But he chose to make the plunge. He had waited long enough. However wise or unwise the decision, it took courage—the courage to risk failure. It was finally a sign that Ted had grown up and become adult.

2

The Fading Star: Why Ted Fell

— 1 —

"IN THE autumn of 1979," wrote James D. Barber, "Ted Kennedy floated high above Carter in the polls, a warm Irish super-politician, apparently predestined to be wafted into the White House." Yet by December, less than a month after Ted's declaration, he was not floating and was being called many names but not a "super-politician." By January he was in deep trouble, when "Carter soared above the pack in the greatest recovery of popular support in the history of polling," and by February Ted was very close to being pushed ingloriously out of the contest he had entered so gloriously. What had happened to make his star fade so fast?

The first thing that happened, even before Ted's official announcement in Boston, was his disintegration on the TV screen in plain sight and hearing of millions. If any single event can be said to have wounded Ted's candidacy mortally it was his interview with Roger Mudd of CBS, on November 4, three days before Ted's declaration. Asked about Chappaquiddick, Ted responded in wandering, broken, incoherent phrases that were scarcely sentences. Asked why he would expect the people to choose him as President, he spoke vaguely of his brothers and of leadership, again almost incoherently.

It revived in his viewers all the doubts about Ted and Chap-

176

paquiddick, and it added another dimension of doubt—not only about what he had done, but how he now responded to what he had done.

The second thing that happened was that Jimmy Carter turned into Lazarus and came back from the dead. It came about with the takeover and the seizure of hostages of the American Embassy in Teheran. The American people responded with anger and hurt pride, and Carter struck the right note of firmness about the return of the hostages and concern about their safety, which was the start of his swift road back to grace. The impact of the hostage crisis was reinforced by anger at the Soviet occupation of Afghanistan. Carter performed another miracle of loaves and fishes by turning American defeat and frustration into an unparalleled recovery at the polls.

—— 2 ——

THERE is an illusion still extant in the Kennedy camp that Ted was doing fine until he was wasted by the hostages and Afghanistan. This is too self-serving an account. Well before the hostages, Ted had begun his downward dive. "It turned out," Barber wrote, "that he had no convincing answers to questions about either his own checkered past or his nation's checkered future."

There was in effect a moratorium of several months on campaign discussions of the hostages, but it operated equally on Ted and the other candidates. The others, Republicans and Democrats alike, either thrived or fell from causes very little related to the moratorium. John Anderson, a Republican almost as liberal in his overall views as Ted, supported Carter on the hostages, yet emerged as a leading candidate despite the moratorium.

On December 2, in a motel room interview with a local TV reporter, fatigued and frustrated, Ted made a blundering attack on the Shah as having run "one of the most violent regimes in the history of mankind." Whatever its degree of truth it was the wrong truth at the wrong time. Unsurprisingly the Iranian militants were jubilant over Ted's remark, which in turn triggered a shock at home. The *New York Post* headlined "Teddy is the Toast of Tehran!" Other papers were less theatrical but just as critical. Ted's troubles began before the events in Teheran but were intensified by them.

Ted also failed to catch up with the swift changes in the necessities of presidential campaigning. He started low-key, as befitted a Kennedy who was loath to evoke more attacks on the family arrogance. But his talk of "leadership" was at once too vague and vulnerable, and while stressing economic issues he failed to differentiate himself sharply from Carter's economic position. Kennedy made the mistake of setting his sights on the election, where he would need a more centrist and consensus position, instead of on the nomination, for which he needed a sharp media image that would carry over with a cumulative victory effect. He failed to focus on a core position.

To add to Ted's woes, in the midst of the Iowa "caucus" primary, there was a resumption of the Chappaquiddick attacks, with a startling impact. The *Los Angeles Times* did a reassessment of the puzzles and gaps in the Chappaquiddick story, whose results were the more damaging because of its detachment. The *Readers' Digest* and the *Washington Star* found a fresh theme in questioning Ted's story about his rescue effort and his swim across the channel, which led Ted's manager to summon oceanographic experts to Washington for an expert rebuttal of the new material about tides and currents that fatal night. The *Digest* article hurt Ted badly because of the magazine's long championing of the traditional values so deeply rooted in Iowa, as also in New Hampshire and Vermont, Ted's next primary states.

Ted's wretched showing in Iowa was worse than either of his brothers had done in any presidential primaries. It led him and his managers to reassess the campaign. They were evenly divided on whether to continue or to cut losses and pull out. Ted swung the balance in favor of continuing. A Kennedy can't be a quitter, he felt. He cut the staff, reorganized the campaign finances, and rethought his strategy. Like the decision to enter the campaign, the decision to continue it in the face of adversity took courage and tenacity.

It became a problem of finding a new and more sharply focused campaign theme. Ted found it finally in an anti-draft stand and anti-inflation plan that proposed a Galbraithian program of total controls over prices, wages, profits, and interest rates. With inflation well into double digit figures this stance became his chief campaign asset. It took precedence over foreign policy, where Ted was mostly waiting either for breaks in his luck or policy blunders by Carter, like the one that came early in March with the Administration's vote against Israel on a UN Resolution on occupied territories. The question was whether Ted could transform the swiftly changing events into delegate victories before the convention in August.

— 3 —

HIS biggest problem—the perception of his character and his past —was underscored by the revolution taking place in the process of selecting presidential candidates. For more than ever it had become a highly personalized process, with the white light of media exposure and the omnivorous hunger for new, sensational material. This had operated in the Kennedys' favor in the past, because the focus was on their personal and political glamour. But it operated against Ted now as the focus shifted to his personal qualities of character and trust, which distracted attention from what he said and the positions he took.

Thus Ted Kennedy, in the 1980 campaign, was undone by a combination of Chappaquiddick, Carter, and the TV primaries system. The primaries were no longer preliminary testings looking toward the national convention, as they had been in the past.

They became in themselves a protracted state-by-state convention in which the voters in effect become the delegates. The agency for this transformation has been TV, which has turned the primaries into a sequence of dramatic town meetings watched by the nation.

The primaries became a new jungle in which the competition is intense and the dropout rate inexorable. On the principle of acceleration, that nothing succeeds like success and nothing fails like failure, the field divides itself—as primary succeeds primary —into the "hot" candidates around whom everyone crowds, and the failures who have not lived up to expectations.

As spring came, Ted found himself, to his dismay, one of the dramatic failures. The galling thing about it was that he was still what he had been. Among close to a dozen candidates from both parties he stood out for his glow and charisma. He brought a feeling of electricity with him that every other candidate had to envy. But once he started to campaign it was not translated into votes and support. The action was not focused on Ted: It was everywhere. Each week had its new heroes and new victims, men on the way either to the summit or the cellar.

It is true that Ted was not running against the Republicans. But the viewers who watched the TV news every night saw the field as a whole. George Bush, Ronald Reagan, John Anderson, each had his day of excitement in the sun. Ted had to run directly only against Carter (Jerry Brown was far behind from the start), but in fact he had to compete for attention with the whole field. Even when he achieved his first success, in Massachusetts, when he won the March primary by a solid majority against Carter, the talk was all about Reagan and Anderson, whose vote margin was not as good as Ted's but who had scored upsets.

For the first time in the history of the dynasty a campaigning Kennedy was one of a field, and had to pay dearly for whatever victory he could wrest from a hostile electorate. What made it worse was that when Ted did get the media attention he needed, in interviews and at press conferences, the intensity of personal exposure on TV—however measured and thoughtful his statements—only seemed to nourish the doubts evoked by Chappaquiddick.

The hardest blow of all came from John Anderson's camp. Like his brothers, Ted had counted on the support of the young voters, especially the liberals in both parties. It was a tradition that wherever and whenever a Kennedy ran, he had a Youth Brigade to canvass for him, man a telephone grid, and give his campaign the air of youthful passion and vision. But in the New Hampshire, Vermont, and Illinois primaries, although Ted did well in attracting youthful supporters, it was John Anderson, not Ted who got their starry-eyed enthusiasm.

It had happened once before, when Bob had to share his Pied Piper role with Gene McCarthy, after the New Hampshire primary. But it was clearer now than ever that a Kennedy could no longer have a monopoly of the magnetizing effect on the young that had been part of the family's political signature.

3

The End of the Legend

— 1 —

SOME future biographer, looking back at the 1980 campaign in a long perspective, may write that in the mid-passage of his life Ted encountered a Dantean lion in his path, and had to grapple with it to discover for himself who he in fact was. He grappled courageously and honorably, although—at present writing—victory still eluded him.

At forty-eight he was still in mid-life, yet in the perception of him by the media there was a whiff of end-of-the-road failure. The fact was, of course, that—whatever the outcome—he was not at the end of his career, and that even the road to the Presidency was not closed off for good.

But if he was indeed to make another try at another time, it would have to be a different Ted who would attempt it, with a different view of himself and his relation to the family legend.

His problem with the voters thus far in the 1980 campaign had to do with the *mistrust* factor. In many of the polls during the campaign, there was a high percentage who said that they wouldn't vote for Ted under any circumstances. It was a credibility question. In a tape Ted did after Iowa, aimed at the New Hampshire viewers, Ted asked them to "believe" his version of the Chappaquiddick incident. But trust is something you can't ask for and get on demand. You have to earn it.

And Ted could earn it only by total candor in the face of Mary Jo Kopechne's fate. "To the living," Charles McCarry has written in a suspense novel about the Kennedys, "one owes consideration, to the dead only the truth."

What Ted owed himself was another form of truth—self-acceptance and self-belief. In his family relationships he had done too many things for others, had them do too many things for him, and lived far too much in the mirror perception of what they thought and expected of him. He has been showing a dawning sense that it is time for him to do something by himself, for himself.

There were many who believed, when Ted declared for the nomination, that he was running because he couldn't say No to his father's expectations. There is a core of truth in it. After Chappaquiddick he had not been able to say No to the circle of his advisers who had gathered around him.

Yet I have to add that the decision to run, however much it may have come from keeping faith with his father, was in part a way of saying Yes to himself, after the three times he had said No. After Iowa, when the prospects were so bleak and his closest advisers were for getting out, Ted again said Yes to himself and stayed in the campaign. It marked the beginning of a new sense of autonomy.

He had much to overcome. His problem from the start until today has been not so much one of wrestling with the authority of one man, his father: It has been a probing of selfhood. Ted led a life whose pressures were multiple and excessive. There have been too many fathers, too many times of decision when the decision came not from him but from them, too controlling a set of parents who made their love too conditional, too intense a family with too competitive a set of demands, too much happening to him, too many tragedies, too many damaging memories.

— 2 —

THE remarkable fact about Ted is the strength he has shown as a survivor. His testings have been brutal. He did not so much overcome them as last them out. Yet with each new scrape and blow Ted showed the resilience to gather his energies and go on. There was no breakdown, not even after Bob's death, when Ted suffered a period of great confusion.

It was in that period that Chappaquiddick happened—the closest to something that shook him to the roots of his being. From that too he could have retrieved himself in time if there had not been a dismal failure of judgment, in his own response and that of his advisers, to add to the dismal failure of character in the event itself.

Ted had to pay heavily for being the youngest and late-born child because it meant that from the start he was swathed in layers of protectiveness. This lasted even after he was grown up. There was always someone to play the protective role of brother or father or both—until Bob's death, when everyone he had leaned on was gone and he had to play all the roles himself. It was a scary thing to stand alone. The thing that was hard to learn was that he was no longer accountable to the dead but to himself.

It isn't easy to live your life in the ghost-filled house of your memories. Ted has had to come to terms with the ghosts of his dead heroes. There were of course differences between their hero roles. His father was the *hero-as-founder.* His brother Jack was the *hero-as-President,* but also as martyr. His brother Bob was the *hero-as-activist* and as *might-have-been-President,* and again as martyr. As for Ted, he may have seen himself only as the *hero-as-brother,* which would scarcely be a heroic enough role. It would be a great temptation to fill out his role by the *hero-as-potential-President,* perhaps even—the thought kept cropping up—as potential martyr.

—— 3 ——

TED is not the sort who dwells on death or gets morbid about the death threats. Yet he has told reporters, "All I want, if someone's going to blow my head off . . . I just want one swing at him first. I just don't want to get it from behind."

Before he entered as presidential candidate there were some editorial suggestions that he ought to run a low-danger campaign, substituting high media visibility for the traditional one-to-one handshaking and flesh-pressing campaign. It was prudent advice, but impossible to carry out. During the high points of his rise in the polls the "you-know-what" theme of possible death was on everyone's mind. When his campaign started the Kennedy caravan contained, in addition to several hundred reporters and the detail of security men, an intensive-care ambulance and a car with a bomb-sniffing dog. This sense of danger to be met fitted in with the dark part of the Kennedy legend.

Yet it doesn't fit with Ted's temperament or his image. Jackie Kennedy blurted out a presentiment of Bob's death, because he had stirred so much hatred. Of the three brothers Bob was the most polarizing, Ted the least. Bob evoked hate, fear, loyalty, love, in abundant measure. Ted evokes enthusiasm (for a time before he declared there was a surge of "Teddymania"), or he evokes dislike and mistrust, but there is little of either committed love or hate. True, he generates an intense energy in a crowd, but he is not as elemental as Bob, nor does he evoke the elemental emotions.

The distinction to make is that Ted is not himself a heroic figure, but has become deeply involved in the myths clustering around the family. In the popular mind therefore he has been absorbed into legend and myth.

— 4 —

ONE is Camelot. As legend it was a latecomer, and didn't take shape until after John Kennedy's death. The three people responsible for it were his widow, Jackie, Theodore H. White, and Alan Jay Lerner.

White has told the story movingly in his memoir, of how Jackie summoned him to Hyannisport a week after the funeral, to ask his help in getting John F. Kennedy to be remembered by history. She didn't mean history as it is written by "bitter old men," she said, but the kind that "belongs to heroes." She didn't want this hero to be forgotten.

She told of the nights when his back hurt and he couldn't go to sleep, and she would get out of bed and play him, on a ten-year-old Victrola, his favorite song from *Camelot:* "Don't let it be forgot/That once there was a spot/For one brief shining moment that was known as Camelot." She went on to say how deeply Jack loved history. "History made Jack what he was . . . this lonely little boy, sick so much of the time, reading in bed, reading the Knights of the Round Table."

She carried through her mission imaginatively and well, and White did his work well, and the story in *Life* swept a nation that had watched, four days running, as the assassination story and the funeral unrolled on the screen, a weekend saturated with the making of myth. As with Abe Lincoln, it was the death of the hero, not his life, that triggered the emotions that turned him into myth. What Jackie Kennedy did for John Kennedy was to find a historical metaphor that invested the Kennedy administration and the all-too-brief Kennedy years with a golden haze of romance.

Some of it was true, in the hard historical sense of the truth, much of it was not. But a legend like this takes on a life of its own —historical truth or not—because people want to believe in it so that their everyday lives and the grimy traffic of politics can find some passion larger than life through it.

Another episode, this time recounted by Alan Jay Lerner,

who had written the lyrics of the song that Jack Kennedy loved to listen to, completes the mythmaking story. After the funeral, at a performance of *Camelot* in Chicago, the theme song that Jack had loved was played. When it was over there was a moment of silence, and then from a corner of the theater there were audible sobs, then more, and soon a sound of sobbing like a wave swept through the audience. More than for a dead President they were sobbing for a collective dream that "for one brief shining moment" had surfaced in the American consciousness.

— 5 —

IT was an extraordinary case study of the making of a contemporary myth, through the collaboration of these three. Yet myths cannot be contrived. There has to be the basic human experience there, ready to be used. How can we doubt the reality of myths, or the need—and indeed healthiness—of releasing in ourselves through some fabled larger-than-life narrative, the drives and yearnings that reside deep within us, and have existed in the whole human experience?

The Camelot story as enacted in the White House had no Lancelot pure of heart, and Jack Kennedy was scarcely King Arthur, and some of the recent research has unearthed aspects of moral squalor rather than glory in the Administration. Yet James M. Burns, quite aware of the shortcomings, rightly insists that Camelot was more than a *legend:* It was a *legacy*—one that has been bequeathed to Ted. The legacy is a dream of what a national Administration under a talented leader can be like, if he has vision and can communicate it to the people.

Yet the legacy—the dream of what might have been and can still be—is only one phase of the legend. Another was the *dynasty* principle, which Joe Kennedy strove to set up and Jack made concrete with his success, and with the dynasty the principle of *hierarchy:* whose turn it was to command the family and aim to command the nation. From there it moved into another phase, of *destiny:* When Bob maneuvered and fought to take his brother's place he was seeking to act out the family destiny. When he too was killed, the vision of destiny was merged with the vision of *death,* and around that too there clustered the mystique of the inevitable.

From legend to legacy, from dream to dynasty, to destiny, to death: The makings of a full-blown myth came together in the tangled threads of the Kennedy story. I have tried to trace it, in its turns and windings, in the course of these pages. It is a myth that Ted had no major hand in making, but it is one that he was expected to take over and in some way to round out. It may prove too heavy a weight for him to bear, but there is no other national political figure in America who is linked with anything like it. That forms at once Ted's appeal and his problem.

Is it true, as Leon Edel has suggested, that each of us, somewhere on the fringes of his daily consciousness, has a secret life myth? I would guess that Ted's has been to be his brother Jack —to have Jack's sharp intelligence and his capacity with words, to live out the Faustian dream that Jack lived out of summit power along with Helen of Troy, to add to it the social passion that Bob possessed more than Jack, and to repay the tacit promise he gave his father of completing Jack's and Bob's work.

Instead of that glowing secret life myth there is the broken myth that Ted has had to face. Instead of the effortless grace with which Jack moved through life there was the blunder of Chappaquiddick—like the Mardi Gras figure of Death chasing Folly around a pole—that broke his life in two, so that nothing has been the same since.

Yet one must add the new resilience, and the movement toward becoming an adult, and facing his own reality, not that of others. Thinking about Ted, at the end of our long journey together, I think of what Crazy Jane said in the Yeats poem: "Nothing can be sole or whole/That has not been rent."

EPILOGUE

As I write this, in the early spring of 1980, Ted Kennedy has not withdrawn from the presidential contest nor wholly given up hope of winning it, although his prospects are pretty dim, his mood chastened, and his image tarnished.

I shall not try to read his political future. Yet I venture some observations in the light of what has emerged from this study.

• Ted showed in the 1980 Massachusetts primary that he still has a solid home base. He will run again in 1982 for another Senate term. He will use his Senate role in the intervening years —and those in the calculable future—to stake out political and economic positions that will continue him as a major influence on national opinion.

• That influence is unlikely to swerve much from the basic liberal pattern that Ted has developed. Given the erratic turns of his life, the element of stability in it has been his liberal doctrine, and it will continue to be. He will make changes in it as political realism may require. But basically he will emulate a member of an earlier Massachusetts political dynasty, John Quincy Adams, who had his place in the sun as President, then went back to his seat in the House of Representatives and remained to guard the citadel of enlightened Whig doctrine.

• But I don't write off Ted's possible presidential future. In fact, given the volatile nature of the 1980 campaign, there is every chance that Jimmy Carter's shifting fortunes may take a plunge, and that Ted—as the only alternative to Carter—may be the beneficiary. In that event the struggle would go to the convention floor, and in a rough Kennedy-Carter melee, Kennedy could emerge with a creditable showing, perhaps even with a victory.

If that doesn't happen, then at forty-eight he has another three, perhaps four, chances to make another try at the nomination. Nothing has been more vividly illustrated by recent American history than its unexpected swings of leadership, mood, and direction.

• Under either Democratic or Republican Administrations in the 1980's, Ted is bound to function best as a continuing leader of the opposition—a role that few have played in recent American history. People will pay heed to his attacks on prevailing policies even when they have not voted for him.

• No new leadership of stature has emerged in recent years in the Democratic Party. Jimmy Carter has functioned as President but not as party leader. The very fact of Ted being available, as a Kennedy, has stifled the emergence of others.

• Chappaquiddick is unlikely to be resolved as a public mystery. But it is also unlikely to last forever. A time may come when people will feel that—punished and chastened by having been denied the nomination—Ted deserves another look and a second assessment.

• For some time Ted will be, for his party and the people, the road not taken. He will thus remain the symbol of an alternative road, which he can keep alive by a steady, sustained stream of policy statements and new options. In a crisis era for Americans, in the 1980's and 1990's, he can fulfill an important leadership function even if he never gets to be President.

BIBLIOGRAPHY

I list here some basic books on Ted and the Kennedy family. For more specific references in the text see the notes to each chapter and section below.

I   On Edward M. Kennedy the crucial books are:
Burns, James MacGregor. *Edward Kennedy and the Camelot Legacy.* New York: Norton, 1976.
David, Lester. *Ted Kennedy: Triumphs and Tragedies.* New York: Grosset & Dunlap, 1972.
Hersh, Burton. *The Education of Edward Kennedy: A Family Biography.* New York: Morrow, 1972.
Honan, William H. *Ted Kennedy: Profile of A Survivor.* New York: Manor, 1972.

II   On Joseph P. Kennedy and the origins of the Kennedy family:
Beschloss, Michael R. *Kennedy and Roosevelt: The Uneasy Alliance.* New York: Norton, 1980.
Koskoff, David E. *Joseph P. Kennedy: A Life and Times.* Englewood Cliffs, N.J.: Prentice-Hall, 1974.
Whalen, Richard J. *The Founding Father.* New York: New American Library, 1964.

III On Rose Kennedy and Joan Kennedy:
Cameron, Gail. *Rose.* New York: Putnam, 1971.

David, Lester. *Joan: The Reluctant Kennedy.* New York: Warner, 1975.

Kennedy, Rose Fitzgerald. *Times to Remember.* New York: Doubleday, 1974.

IV   On the Kennedy brothers and sisters and the family:

Barber, James D. *The Presidential Character,* 2nd. ed. Englewood Cliffs, N.J.: Prentice-Hall, 1977.

Bradlee, Benjamin C. *Conversations with Kennedy.* New York: Norton, 1975.

Buck, Pearl. *The Kennedy Women.* New York: Cowles, 1970.

Burns, James MacGregor. *John Kennedy: A Political Profile.* New York: Harcourt Brace, 1960.

Clinch, Nancy Gager. *The Kennedy Neurosis: A Psychological Portrait of an American Dynasty.* New York: Grosset & Dunlap, 1973.

De Toledano, Ralph. *RFK: The Man Who Would be President.* New York: Putnam, 1967.

Lasky, Victor. *JFK: The Man and the Myth.* New Rochelle, N.Y.: Arlington, 1966.

Newfield, Jack. *Robert Kennedy: A Memoir.* New York: Dutton, 1969.

Schlesinger, Arthur M., Jr. *Robert Kennedy and His Times.* New York: Ballantine, 1979.

Schlesinger, Arthur M., Jr. *A Thousand Days: John F. Kennedy in the White House.* New York: Houghton Mifflin, 1965.

Sorensen, Theodore C. *Kennedy.* New York: Harper, 1965.

Sorensen, Theodore C. *The Kennedy Legacy.* New York: Macmillan, 1969.

Van den Heuvel, William and Gwirtzman, Milton. *On His Own: Robert Kennedy 1964–68.* New York: Doubleday, 1970.

Note: There is a forthcoming book by Herbert Parmet, *Jack,* first volume to be published by Dial, New York, in 1980.

Doris Kearns is also at work on a three-generational story of the family.

V   On Chappaquiddick:
    For the source material:
Boyle, James A., Justice. Report. Inquest re Mary Jo Kopechne. Docket No. 15220. Dukes County, SS, District Court. February 18, 1970.

Inquest into the Death of Mary Jo Kopechne. Edgartown, Mass. 5 vols. January 5–8, 1970. Docket No. 15220.

For secondary material:

Auffray, Jean Paul. Investigation Series. *New York Post,* July 9, 1979.

Barron, John. "Chappaquiddick: The Still Unanswered Questions." *Readers' Digest,* February 1980.

Cadden, Vivian. "What Happened at Chappaquiddick." *McCall's,* August 1974.

Dunne, John Gregory. "On the Matter of Chappaquiddick." *New West,* December 3, 1979.

Investigation Series. *Washington Star,* January 15, 1980.

Olsen, Jack. *The Bridge at Chappaquiddick.* New York: Little, Brown, 1970.

Ostrow, Ronald J. and Jackson, Robert L. Investigative Series. *Los Angeles Times,* December 23, 24, 1979.

Rust, Zad. *Teddy Bare: The Last of the Kennedy Clan.* Belmont, Mass.: Western Islands, 1971.

Sherrill, Robert. "Chappaquiddick + 5." *The New York Times,* July 14, 1974.

Sherrill, Robert. *The Last Kennedy.* New York: Dial, 1976.

Tedrow, Richard, and Tedrow, Thomas. *Death at Chappaquiddick.* Ottawa, Ill.: Green Hill, 1976.

Thomas, Jo. "Gaps Found in Chappaquiddick Phone Data." Investigative Report. *New York Times,* March 15, 1980.

Note: There is a forthcoming book on Chappaquiddick by Ladislas Farago to be published by Avon, New York, in 1980.

VI   On the Kennedy legend:
Burns, James MacGregor. *Edward Kennedy and the Camelot Legacy.* New York: Norton, 1976.
Decter, Midge. "Kennedyism Again." *Commentary,* December 1978.
Lapham, Lewis. "Edward Kennedy and the Romance of Death." *Harper's,* December 1979.
Roberts, Steven V. "Ted Kennedy: Haunted by the Past." *The New York Times Magazine,* February 3, 1980.
Taylor, Anne Fleming. "The Kennedy Mystique." (2 parts.) *The New York Times,* June 17, 1979.

VII   On the 1979–80 campaign:
Honan, William H. "The Kennedy Network." *The New York Times Magazine* (cover story), November 5, 1979.

VIII   For Ted's own books:
Kennedy, Edward M. *Decisions for a Decade.* New York: New American Library, 1968.
Kennedy, Edward M. *Our Day and Generation: The Words of Edward M. Kennedy.* Ed. by Henry Steele Commager, with Foreword by Archibald MacLeish. New York: Simon and Schuster, 1979.

NOTES AND REFERENCES

CHAPTER I

PRIMAL FATHER AND BAND OF BROTHERS

I have relied most heavily in this chapter on Whalen, Hersh, Burns, Koskoff, and Beschloss.

1/ The Family: Rooted and Invented

The material in the above books on the Fitzgerald family has been supplemented by Rose Kennedy, *Times to Remember* (New York: Doubleday, 1974). I am indebted to E. Digby Baltzell, *Puritan Boston and Quaker Philadelphia* (New York: Free Press, 1980), not only for the quotes from Henry Adams but also for the contrasts between the earlier New England oligarchy and the newcomer elite.

2/ Joseph Kennedy's Grand Design

I am indebted to Koskoff and Whalen and especially to Beschloss. For Joe Kennedy's remarks about the Fitzgeralds see Koskoff 8, 22. For Gloria Swanson relationship see Koskoff 35–6. For Thorstein Veblen on industrialists and financiers see my Introduction to the *Portable Veblen* (New York: Viking, 1958). For the magnificos and the puritans among American businessmen, see my *America as a Civilization* (New York: Simon & Schuster, 1957). For my account of the relations between Joe

Kennedy and Franklin Roosevelt I have profited greatly from Beschloss. The most severe psycho-historical view of Joe Kennedy and his motivation is Nancy Gager Clinch, *The Kennedy Neurosis* (New York: Grosset & Dunlap, 1973) with a Foreword by Bruce Mazlish. The remark by Joe Kennedy about Roosevelt as the "next President" was made to Jeremiah Milbank in 1930 and is found in Whalen, 113. Joe Kennedy's book *I'm for Roosevelt* was published by Reynal & Hitchcock (New York) in 1936; it may have been largely ghost-written by Arthur Krock. The "too dangerous to have around" is from Koskoff, 117 and Beschloss, 157. For the ambassadorship as an FDR "joke" ("the greatest joke in the world," FDR called it) see Beschloss, 157. For "He's a pain in the neck" see Whalen, 213. Joe Kennedy's return from London in 1940 and the dinner-party scene at the White House are best described in Beschloss, 215–19. For the Kennedy endorsement speech on October 29 see Beschloss, 219–21. For the Louis Lyons interview in the Boston *Globe* see Whalen, 342–3.

3/   Patriarch, Great Mother, Band of Brothers

For the archetypal structure of family relationships I have been helped by Norman O. Brown, *Love's Body* (New York: Vintage, 1966), F. J. Sulloway, *Freud, Biologist of the Mind* (New York: Basic, 1979), and Erich Neumann, *The Great Mother* (Princeton, N.J.: Princeton 1972). The material on Rose Kennedy is based on her memoirs and on Gail Cameron, *Rose.* The "trust fund" discussion with Hearst will be found in Beschloss, 64. The vignettes of Joe Kennedy as stern father are from Hersh, 29, 39. The description of Joe Kennedy Jr. as "heir-presumptive" relies on Hank Searls, *The Lost Prince: Young Joe, the Forgotten Kennedy* (New York: New American Library, 1969). For discussion on *agon* as a force in growing up see my *Values in Education* (Phi Delta Kappa, 1976) 28, 33, 119. On Joe Kennedy Jr.'s dissenting voice against FDR at the 1940 convention see Burns, 30. For the estimate of Joe Kennedy's wealth I have relied on Kosloff, 322.

CHAPTER II

SHAPING A KENNEDY

For suggestions on the developmental life cycle underlying this chapter I am indebted to Erik Erikson, *Identity and the Life Cycle: Selected Papers* (New York: International Universities Press, 1959); Paul Roazen, *Erik H. Erikson: The Power and Limits of a Vision* (New York: Free Press, 1976); John S. Dunne, *The City of the Gods* (New York: Macmillan, 1965); Daniel J. Levinson, *The Seasons of a Man's Life* (New York, Knopf, 1978), and George E. Vaillant, *Adaptation to Life* (New York: Little, Brown, 1977).

1/ The Late-Born

James Burns's phrase "the late-born" is from his *Edward Kennedy and the Camelot Legacy,* 71. My stream-of-consciousness sequence of Ted's boyhood memories owes much to Whalen, Hersh, Burns. For Ted's multiple schooling see Burns, 36, and Hersh, 38. The Henry James remark is from his memoirs *Notes from a Son and Brother.* For the circumstances of Joe Kennedy Jr.'s death in the bombing raid the fullest discussion is in Koskoff, 334, 374. For the priests coming to tell Joe Kennedy Sr. of his son's death see Hersh, 35. Ted's toast to his absent brother, see Hersh, 47. For Ted's years at Milton Academy see Burns and Hersh.

2/ Moratorium: Rebelling, Probing Limits, Expiation

The concept of adolescence as a "moratorium" is developed in Erikson. I have also profited from Barbara M. and Philip R. Newman, *Development Through Life* (Homewood, Ill.: Dorsey, rev. ed., 1979). For Bob's adolescent moods see Arthur M. Schlesinger, Jr., *Robert F. Kennedy and His Times* (New York: Ballantine, 1979) and Hersh, 69–72. For the postwar "Beat Generation" mood at Harvard see Hersh, 79–80, and Burns, 43. For Ted's dating at college see Burns, 48. The fullest discussion of the "Spanish exam" episode is in Hersh, 75–81. For the Army experience see Burns, 44–6.

3/   Finding His Vocation, Winning His Spurs

For Henri Bergson on concept of time I have used the discussion by Stuart Hughes, *Consciousness and Society* (New York: Random, 1961). For insights into the stages from adolescence into early manhood, I rely upon Erikson, Levinson, Newman and Newman, and also Calvin S. Hall and Vernon J. Nordby, *A Primer of Jungian Psychology* (New York: Mentor, 1973). Ted's summer in the Berber area in North Africa is described in Hersh, 99, and Jack Kennedy's speech on Algeria from Ted's material see Burns, 50. Jack's narrow escape from being nominated for Vice-President is discussed in Burns, *John Kennedy: A Political Profile* (New York: Harcourt Brace, 1960). For Ted's law school admittance problems see Burns, 50 and Hersh, 100. His law school career is discussed fully in Hersh and Burns, including the moot court competition and the police episode. The latter episode is also discussed by William Safire in *The New York Times* (10/29/79). For Ted's risk-taking in various sports see Burns, 47, and Hersh, 103. For Ted's courtship and marriage see Burns, 52. On the vocation of politics I build on Max Weber's thinking. On the relation between leader and demos, I have drawn on two very diverse books—Norman Brown, *Love's Body* (New York: Random, 1968), and James M. Burns, *Leadership* (New York: Harper Colophon, 1978). For Jack's 1952 Senate campaign, and Ted's role in it, see Burns, 104, and for Ted's role in Jack's presidential campaign see Hersh, 138.

4/   Becoming His Own Man: The Path to the Senate

For the concept of "becoming one's own man" see Daniel Levinson, *The Seasons of A Man's Life,* and for Jung's thinking on individuation see Hall and Nordby, *A Primer of Jungian Psychology.* For the Inauguration and the Inaugural speech see Arthur M. Schlesinger, Jr., *A Thousand Days,* "Prologue" (New York: Houghton Mifflin, 1965). A convenient reprint of the Inaugural Address is in the *Annals of America: 1493–1973* (Encyclopedia Brittanica, Vol. 18) 5–11. For Rose Kennedy's remark about "evening the score" see Whalen, 434. For a discussion of the Attorney-General appointment and the working relationship of Jack and Bob the fullest treatment is in Arthur M. Schlesinger, *Robert F. Kennedy,* 250–55. The "you hold your balls" story is in Theodore H. White, *In Search of History,* 496. On the family efforts to hold Jack's Senate seat for Ted, see Hersh, 147–49, and Burns, 74. For the "Now It's Ted's turn" episode, see Burns, 75. For Filmer, Hobbes, and Locke on primogeniture and the equal division of inheritance, see Norman Brown, *Love's Body,* Chapter 1 on "Liberty," which also gave me some suggestions for my discussion of the hierarchical principle in the Kennedy family. The controversy over Ted's senatorial campaign and the details of the campaign itself are best discussed in Hersh and Burns. The "If your name were Edward Moore" episode is in Burns, 90. For the "Princely Effect" in Ted's Senate election, see Burns, 91. Joe Kennedy's stroke is discussed in Whalen. For the organization and tactics of Kennedy campaigns, see Murray Levin, *Kennedy Campaigning* (New York: Beacon, 1960).

CHAPTER III

THE TRIUMPH AND SAVAGING OF THE HOUSE OF KENNEDY

1/   The Magus and the Brothers

Arthur M. Schlesinger's description of Joe Kennedy is from *Robert F. Kennedy and His Times,* 12. I have taken my Magus and Faustus figures in part from Oswald Splengler, *Decline of the West,* in part from E. M. Butler's studies of the Faustus legend. For Daedalus and the "Fabulous Artificer" see James Joyce's *Ulysses,* and for the archetypal relations between father and sons I owe much to Brown, *Love's Body,* Sigmund Freud, *Totem and Taboo* (1913), and Frank J. Sulloway, *Freud: Biologist of the Mind* (New York: Basic, 1979), especially Chapters 10 and 11. The divergence of the Kennedy brothers from their father in their thinking is nowhere discussed at length: I have pieced it together from fragments in Koskoff, Burns, Hersh, and Schlesinger. For the story of Ted on his ski jump see Burns, 66. For Joe Kennedy's last assertions of authority: on the choice of Lyndon Johnson as Vice-President, see Koskoff, 423–4, Schlesinger, *A Thousand Days,* 45–57, Schlesinger, *Robert Kennedy,* 222–231, and on "Ted's turn" for the Senate see Burns, 75.

2/   Death of the Brother/Father

For Ted's initial Senate years see Burns, 100, 240–4. On Ted's response to the news of Jack's assassination and breaking of news to his father, see Hersh, 184–7. For Jack's funeral, and the role of Ted and the other Kennedys in it, I owe much to Arthur Schlesinger's account in *A Thousand Days,* 1031, and especially in *Robert F. Kennedy,* 658, 665, and Hersh, 187. In comparing the impact of Jack's death on the two brothers I have profited from Schlesinger on *Robert F. Kennedy* and from Hersh. Bob's sentence "Three years is better than nothing" is cited in Schlesinger on *Robert F. Kennedy,* 661.

3/   Ted and Bob: The New Axis, the Final Death

The Peter Maas story is from Arthur Schlesinger, *Robert F. Kennedy,* 661. The inscription on Jack's inaugural gift of a cigarette case to Bob comes from Olsen, 19. For my discussion of Bob's inner struggle after Jack's death, and his feud with Lyndon Johnson, I have relied on Schlesinger. For Ted's and Bob's relations as Senators, and their shaping of a political position and attitude, I have used Burns, 130, 333–7, and Honan, 33, 88. For Ted's plane crash and his political education at the hospital see Burns, 120–5. For the successive phases of Bob's decision on the 1968 presidential campaign and Ted's role in it, Arthur Schlesinger on *Robert F. Kennedy* has the fullest account, 883–904. On the revolutionary turbulence of the 1960's I have used Milton Viorst, *Fire in the Streets: America in the 1960's* (New York: Simon & Schuster, 1979). My discussion of C. Wright Mills and the new intellectual class, as also of Eugene McCarthy and the New Hampshire primary, is indebted to Viorst. Ted's role as manager of Bob's campaign is discussed best in Burns, 142–47. For the tension and the heartbreak of the campaign I have found Hersh, Chapter 8, "Cannonball," most moving.

4/   The Climate of Tragedy and Legend

For Ted's reaction to Bob's killing, Hersh, 330–1, is valuable. It contains Ted's "I'm going to show them what they've done" remark, and Joe Kennedy's grief. I take Geza Roheim's *Eternal Ones of the Dream* from Brown's *Love's Body*. For Ted's eulogy at Bob's funeral see Hersh, 328, and Burns, 147. The rage over the deaths of Martin Luther King and Robert Kennedy, and the burning cities as a funeral pyre for King, are best discussed in Viorst, *Fire in the Streets.*

CHAPTER IV

CHAPPAQUIDDICK: THE SELF-INFLICTED WOUND

1/ On His Own: A Confused Search for a Role

For Ted's confusion after Bob's death I have drawn on Hersh's chapter "Two Summers." The "Fallen Standard" speech was delivered at the Worcester Chamber of Commerce on August 21, 1968. Ted's Alaskan trip is described fully in Hersh, 379, which contains also the "they'll shoot my ass off" story.

2/ By the Rude Dyke Bridge

For my discussion of the Chappaquiddick episode I have profited from the section on "Gargan's party" in Hersh, 390, and have used also Jack Olsen, *The Bridge at Chappaquiddick* and Zad Rust, *Teddy Bare: The Last of the Kennedy Clan,* as well as an account given me by Ladislas Farago of his book still in press at this writing, *Worse than a Crime* (New York: Avon, 1980). The other material I have relied on will be found in the fuller bibliography on Chappaquiddick at the start of this note on reading. My reference to Thomas Kuhn is to his *The Structure of Scientific Revolutions,* 2nd, ed. (Chicago: University of Chicago, 1970) where the concept of paradigms is discussed. Ted's Chappaquiddick TV speech is reprinted in Olsen, 245, as well as in Zad Rust, 270–2. Olsen and Burns discuss the responses to the speech.

3/   Thirteen Puzzles: Three and A Half Hypotheses

I have woven together material from all the sources cited in my Chappaquiddick bibliography, but have shaped my own critique and reconstruction, for which I can hold no one else responsible.

4/   Camelot and Chappaquiddick: Myth and Countermyth

Again I have used material from all my Chappaquiddick sources, but my analysis of the role played by the legal process and the judicial agencies is my own. So also is my use of Chappaquiddick as the "dark" countermyth to the myth of Camelot, with an obvious debt to Jungian myth theory. The Schlesinger reference on the "iron that entered Ted's soul" is from Burns, 330. I have discussed Schlesinger's "continuing expiation" theory with him in personal conversation, but again my interpretation is my own.

CHAPTER V

SENATE HARBOR, PRESIDENTIAL SEA

1/   The Good Senator

The best discussion of Ted as Senator is in Burns and in Hersh. My discussion of Kennedy's doctrinal liberalism should be seen against the background of some of my other writings on liberalism as an ideology, including *It Is Later Than You Think* (New York: Viking 1938), *Ideas Are Weapons* (New York: Viking, 1939), and *America as a Civilization* (New York: Simon & Schuster, 1957). See also my article, "Liberalism" in the *Encyclopedia Britannica*. I have distilled here some views about his positions which I have developed in a number of my columns over the years. For more detailed studies of his record see Timothy B. Clark, "Kennedy's Socio-Economic Record," *Journal of the Institute for Socio-Economic Studies,* Spring 1980, Vol. V, No. 1, and Joshua Maravchik,

"Kennedy's Foreign Policy: What the Record Shows," *Commentary,* Dec. 1979, 3*ff.* See also an exchange about the latter in the readers' columns, *Commentary,* March 1980, 4*ff.* For the double episode of Ted's victory and defeat in the contest for Democratic Whip, the best sources are Hersh and Burns.

2/ Intimacy Relations

I take the Eros concept from Sigmund Freud, *Civilization and Its Discontents* (1930), as representing not only the principle of sexuality and love but also of life-affirmation in the struggle with the Death principle, Thanatos. I use "Intimacy Relations" as the whole cluster of relationships gathering around Eros. On Rose Kennedy in addition to her memoir, *Times to Remember,* and Gail Cameron, *Rose,* see Doris Faber, *The Mothers of American Presidents* (New York: New American Library, 1968). I have also found Hersh, Koskoff, and Burns helpful. Ted's description of his mother—"She could diagram a sentence"—will be found in his dedicatory page to her in his book, *Our Day and Generation: The Words of Edward M. Kennedy* (New York: Simon & Schuster, 1979). Her statement about "raising a great son or daughter" is from *Times to Remember.* Joe Kennedy's comment—"It's the best thing that ever happened to you"—is discussed in Hersh. Jack Kennedy's affair in San Francisco is discussed in Herbert Parmet's forthcoming book, *Jack* (New York, Dial, 1980). My own discussion of the relationship of Eros and power in John Kennedy's life—as also in the lives of Franklin Roosevelt, Dwight Eisenhower, and Lyndon Johnson—appears in my article on "Eros and Power" in *Playboy* (December 1978). Ted's extramarital relationships are dealt with, from a feminist standpoint, in Suzannah Lessard's article, "Kennedy's Woman Problem—Women's Kennedy Problem," in *Washington Monthly* (December 1979). For my discussion of Joan Kennedy I have used material in Hersh and Burns, as also Lester David, *Joan: The Reluctant Kennedy* (New York: Warner paper, 1975), and Kandy Stroud, "Joan Kennedy: Woman Under Pressure," *Ladies Home Journal* (September 1974). Clinch on *The Kennedy Neurosis* also contains discussions of Rose Kennedy and of the Kennedy daughters.

3/ Why Ted Slept: 1968, 1972, 1976

My basic material in this section comes from Burns, Hersh and Honan, but I have brought it together in an interpretive pattern for which they are not responsible. The meeting of Allard Lowenstein with Ted in the hospital elevator is in Honan, 129–30. The Daley remark, "Jack Kennedy knew how to count" is in Hersh, 349. The discussions between Steve Smith and Daley, and Smith's estimate that Ted "could have had it" are in Hersh, 347–9. The Worcester "Fallen Standard" speech is in Hersh, 340. Ted's "this was Bobby's year" is in Hersh, 352. Ted's estimate that he "could have won the nomination but not the election" is from Burns, 152, and Ted's comment, "I just didn't have the stomach for it" from Hersh, 351.

For the 1972 campaign I have relied in part on Honan, *Profile of a Survivor*, based on reportage and interviews with Ted during that year, and in part on Burns, who interviewed Ted in December 1971.

For the 1976 campaign, the story of the "Great Renunciation," in 1974, is best told in Burns.

CHAPTER VI

ACTING OUT THE LEGEND: THE CAMPAIGN OF 1979–80

The material for this chapter comes necessarily out of transient newspaper and magazine sources during the brief period it covers. I give specific citations only where they stand out from the mass of news reports and commentaries.

1/ Gage of Battle: Why Ted Ran

The shifting figures on the Carter and Kennedy poll rating are from Gallup and Harris polls through the entire period from the spring of 1979 to the spring of 1980. I have also used the CBS News and *The New York Times* poll. Ted's formula answer about supporting Carter dates from January 1979. The "I'll whip his ass" statement by President Carter was widely reported in the press in mid-June as was Ted's response.

2/   *The Fading Star: Why Ted Fell*

The quotes from James D. Barber are from his book, *The Pulse of Politics* (New York: Norton, 1980), and as excerpted in *Psychology Today,* March 1980. The Roger Mudd interview with Ted is available from a CBS transcript. I take the account of Ted's motel room TV interview, with its attack on the Shah of Iran, from Peter Ross Range, "Travels with Teddy," *Playboy,* April 1980. For the citations to the *Los Angeles Times* and *Washington Star* pieces on Chappaquiddick which appeared during the campaign, see the bibliography on Chappaquiddick. John Barron's "Chappaquiddick: The Still Unanswered Questions," in *Readers' Digest,* February 1980, received wide media publicity. Ted's Iowa campaign was described by Elizabeth Drew in an article in *The New Yorker,* "1980: Kennedy," Feb. 4, 1980. The *Village Voice* published some vivid reportage on Ted's New Hampshire campaign from which my account of his ambulance and security entourage is taken.

3/   *The End of the Legend*

Of the growing mass of material on the Kennedy legend, some of it cited in my bibliography, I have found Burns, Roberts, and Lapham particularly helpful. For my analysis of the larger myths I have learned much from Otto Rank, *The Myth of the Birth of the Hero and other Essays,* ed. by Philip Freund (New York: Vintage, 1959), and from Ernest Becker, *The Denial of Death* (New York: Free Press, 1973), which is an elaboration of Rank's thinking. My discussion of Camelot is heavily indebted to Theodore H. White, *In Search of History* (New York: Warner paper, 1978), Chapter 11, to Alan Jay Lerner, *The Street Where I Live* (New York: Norton, 1978), pp. 250–3, and to James M. Burns, *Edward Kennedy and the Camelot Legacy.*

INDEX

209